OLYSLAGER AUTO LIBRARY

American Cars of the 1950s

compiled by the OLYSLAGER ORGANISATION
edited by Bart H. Vanderveen

FREDERICK WARNE
London and New York

THE OLYSLAGER AUTO LIBRARY

This book is one of a growing range of titles on major transport subjects.
Titles published so far include:

Copyright © Olyslager Organisation NV 1973
Published by Frederick Warne (Publishers) Ltd
Reprinted 1975, 1977, 1978

Library of Congress Catalog Card No. 73-75031

ISBN 0 7232 1707 6

Filmset and printed in Great Britain
by BAS Printers Limited, Over Wallop, Hampshire

INTRODUCTION

Like the preceding volumes 'American Cars of the 1930s' and 'American Cars of the 1940s', this book is set out on a year-by-year basis, presenting typical examples of cars produced in North America during 1950–59. Some models of South American origin are included also. During the decade the average 'regular' American car was transformed from the straightforward immediate post-war model to the tail-finned dual-headlight giant. Automatic transmission, power brakes and steering, air conditioning and other refinements became commonplace. The smaller manufacturers soon introduced smaller, less complicated and more economical cars and the number of foreign small cars imported, notably Volkswagen, grew dramatically. The 'big three', General Motors, Ford and Chrysler, had to counteract but it was not until 1959 that they unveiled their economy cars which became known as the 'compacts'. These were in addition to their 'regulars' and were later supplemented by 'intermediates' and 'sub-compacts'. Some 'sports type' models made their appearance also, notably the Chevrolet Corvette, the Ford Thunderbird and the Studebaker Hawk.

It was also a decade of expansion of the advertising men's vocabulary. As one British journalist put it: "The American Industry appears to have developed to a fine pitch the technique of evolving names that are not only arresting or attractive, but also have a fascinating pseudo-scientific atmosphere that is impressive". These names were evolved for automatic transmissions (Hydra-Matic, Ultramatic, Fordomatic, Dynaflow, Power-glide, PowerFlite, TorqueFlite, etc.), power brakes (Easamatic, Power Smooth, etc.) and other convenience features. Engines were given impressive names too: Rocket, Safety Surge, Hurricane, Blue Flame, Firepower, Skypower, Powermaster, Dual Powerflyte, to list a few.

During the period under review some drastic changes took place in automotive history. The Kaiser and Frazer cars disappeared. Willys' post-war passenger cars came and went, as did Ford's 'white elephant', the Edsel. Hudson, Nash and Packard, once well-established 'independents' could not hold their own and in spite of mergers these makes disappeared from the scene. What remained eventually were General Motors with Buick, Cadillac, Chevrolet, Oldsmobile and Pontiac; Ford with Ford, Lincoln and Mercury; Chrysler with Chrysler, Dodge, Imperial and Plymouth; and American Motors with Rambler and Jeep.

The quality of the survivors left little to be desired and this was clearly demonstrated by a Canadian hardware salesman who used to trade his car in for a new one every three years. Contemplating the vast profits made by the auto makers he decided to try to make his latest acquisition, a 1957 Chevrolet Bel Air sedan with standard six-cylinder engine, last for at least half a million miles. He saw to it that the car was greased at 1000-mile intervals and maintained properly, by an independent garage. By early 1972 his Chevy had clocked up more than 432,000 miles, a mileage and a timespan during which he would otherwise have had five cars and be on his sixth. The car still had its ("inaudible") original engine, transmission and paint finish, and was free of squeaks and rattles. His motto: "Buy the best-selling model of a quality make's medium-price range, find a conscientious mechanic who is a good diagnostician and stick to him, never skip or skimp a service schedule and use commonsense for the first 250,000 miles".

"American cars", one British user observed, "have a built-in margin of misuse; they are made for a buying public that demands the utmost in terms of performance, styling and gadgetry, but is not prepared to look after them. Anyone who gives them just a little bit of attention gains hands down".

This welcome reliability and durability keeps American cars running, but not the manufacturers' production lines. It is one of the basic reasons why American auto makers are forced to be so fashion-conscious and apply 'built-in obsolescence' by regularly introducing new models and, more often than not, annual facelifts.

Piet Olyslager, MSIA, MSAE, KIVI

1950

With the main exceptions of Buick and Cadillac most United States auto makers continued production of their 1949 models, albeit with distinguishable detail changes. This was hardly surprising since for the 1949 model year they had introduced their first real post-war designs. There was as a consequence little or no reason for extensive changes, especially as the American public continued trading their pre-war cars in for new ones. Buick and Cadillac, as well as Oldsmobile for its 98 Series, had entirely new Fisher bodywork. Other manufacturers, e.g. Chevrolet, Chrysler, DeSoto, Dodge and Pontiac, introduced additional body styles, particularly hardtops, and automatic transmission became available on more models. Sales of new cars in 1950 were over 1½-million units up on the previous year and totalled 6,665,863. This figure was to be exceeded only once during the decade, in 1955, when almost eight million were sold. The Korea hostilities, which started in June 1950, meant that the automotive industry became involved in defence production yet again. Most car and truck manufacturers were awarded contracts for military hardware.

4B Cadillac 61

4A Buick Roadmaster

4C Chevrolet Styleline DeLuxe

4A: **Buick** offered 22 models: seven Series 40 Specials, seven Series 50 Supers and eight top-line Series 70 Roadmasters. The latter had four 'port-holes', the others three. All had 8-in-line OHV engines, with hydraulic valve lifters and CID was 248, 263 and 320 resp. Prices ranged from $1803 to $3433. Buick became the fourth manufacturer to produce more than half a million cars in one year (552,827) and no less than 429,903 of these had the relatively new Dynaflow torque-converter transmission. Shown is the Roadmaster Sedan, Model 72.

4B: **Cadillac** Series 61 Sedan, Model 6169. This year Cadillac produced over 100,000 cars for the first time in its history. There were four lines: Series 61 (122-in wb), 62 (126-in wb), 60S (130-in wb)

and 75 (146¾-in wb, eight-passenger), as well as a 163-in wb ambulance chassis (86). All models had 331 CID V8 engines with hydraulic valve lifters and most were available with Hydra-Matic Drive.

4C: **Chevrolet** Series 2100HK Styleline DeLuxe Sedan, Model 2103. Two- and four-door sedans were also available with fastback (Fleetline DeLuxe Models 2152 and 2153 resp.). Austere versions of most Chevrolet models were in the 1500HJ Special Series. All had the familiar valve-in-head Six engine of 216 CID (235 CID when equipped with the new Powerglide auto.trans.). In 1950 this GM division reached the highest production volume by any auto maker in history with 2,108,273 units. In December the 25-millionth Chevy was made.

5A Chrysler New Yorker

5B Chrysler Imperial

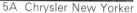

5A : **Chrysler** New Yorker Sedan. Two series were offered : C-48 with 125½-in wb (Royal, Windsor) and C-49 with 131½-in wb (Saratoga, New Yorker, Town & Country). Engines were 250·6 CID Six and 323·5 CID Eight respectively.

5B : **Chrysler** Crown Imperial, Series C-50, with custom-built body by Derham. Luxury car with 145½-in wb and 323·5 CID L-head eight-in-line engine.

5C : **Crosley** Model VC Hotshot Roadster. In at least one country the Crosley mini-cars were known as Crosmobiles, to avoid confusion with the British Crossley. Model VC had 85-in wb, CD Sedans and Wagons 80-in. All had 44 CID 4-cyl. engines.

5D : **DeSoto** had two ranges : S-14 DeLuxe and Custom (shown), both with 236·7 CID L-head Six engine and 125½-in wb. Model availability was three and six resp., not counting some 139½-in wb 8- and 9-pass. models and a taxi. For export there was also the smaller SP-20 Diplomat, basically a Plymouth (q.v.).

5E : **Dodge** Coronet D-34 was top-line model, on 123½-in wb. Other series were Kingsway D-36 (export), Wayfarer D-33 (115-in wb) and Meadowbrook D-34 (123½-in wb). All had L-head Six engines. In the Coronet line there was also a 137½-in wb 8-passenger sedan.

5C Crosley Hotshot

5D DeSoto Custom

5E Dodge Coronet

1950

6A: **Ford** offered 95-bhp Six (OHA) and 100-bhp V8 (OBA) ranges, both with 114-in wb. In each range there were basic (DeLuxe) and more luxurious (Custom) models, and a variety of body styles. Shown is the Series OHA Six DeLuxe Tudor (two-door Sedan), Model 70A.

6B: **Ford** Series OBA V8 Custom Fordor (four-door sedan), Model 73B. The V8 engine was the 239·4 CID 100-bhp L-head. A special 110-bhp engine was available for law enforcement agencies. During 1950 a luxury Tudor, named Crestliner, was announced. Like the Convertible it was available only with V8 engine.

6C: **Frazer** 1950 models were same as in 1949, comprising a four-door Sedan, Model F505, with list price of $2254, a luxurious Model F506 Manhattan Sedan at $2446, and the illustrated Convertible version of the latter at $3110. All were mechanically similar to the Kaiser (q.v.).

6C Frazer

6A Ford Six Deluxe

6D: **Hudson** produced three ranges: Pacemaker (500) and Pacemaker DeLuxe (50A) on 119-in wb with 232 CID engine, Super Six (501) and Eight (503) on 124-in wb with 262 and 254 CID engine resp., and top-line Commodore Six (502) and Eight (504) with wheelbase and engines as Super Six and Eight. All had the 'step-down' Monobilt body-cum-frame design with recessed floor as introduced in 1947 and in-line L-head engines. Shown: Super Six Sedan.

6E: **Kaiser** offerings were same as in 1949: four-door six-seaters with 123½-in wb and Continental 226·2 CID L-head Six engine. Models ranged from a four-door Convertible at $3016 (list price) down to the Special Sedan at $1874. Included were the K501 Traveler (shown) and K502 Vagabond (DeLuxe) sedan-shaped utilities. Entirely new models were introduced in May (see 1951).

6D Hudson Super Six

6B Ford V8 Custom

6E Kaiser Traveler

7A Lincoln Cosmopolitan

7E Oldsmobile 76

7B Mercury

7C Meteor

7D Nash Airflyte

AIRFLYTE CONSTRUCTION
NOW BRINGS YOU 1950'S MOST MODERN CARS!

WITH THE *THRILL* OF NEW SUPER-POWER ENGINES!

ONE SINGLE WELDED UNIT!

Stays new years longer

Nash The Statesman The Ambassador

GREAT CARS SINCE 1902

BETTER LIVING THROUGH BETTER ROADS

7A: **Lincoln** Cosmopolitan, Series OEH, had 336·7 CID L-head V8 and 125-in wb. Two-door Coupé (shown), Convertible and Sedan were available. The lower-priced OEL, with 121-in wb, comprised Coupé and Sport Sedan models.

7B: **Mercury** 1950 models, Series OM, were facelifted 1949s. Again there was a Coupé (Body Type 72, shown), a Sport Sedan (74), a Convertible (76) and a Station Wagon (79). Of the Coupé there were now Standard (72A), DeLuxe (72B) and Custom (72C) variants. All had 118-in wb chassis and 255·4 CID flat-head V8 engine. French Ford Vedette had similar styling features.

7C: **Meteor** (shown) and Monarch were produced in Canada, based on US Ford and Mercury respectively but with different grille and trim features.

7D: **Nash** offered Rambler (new 100-in wb Station Wagon and Convertible), Statesman (112-in wb, DeLuxe, Super, Custom) and Ambassador (121-in wb, Super and Custom). All had Airflyte styling with enclosed front wheels, a 1949–56 Nash feature.

7E: **Oldsmobile** Series 76 Sedan, one of 13 models with 257 CID in-line L-head Six engine. Wheelbase 119½ in.

1950

8A: **Oldsmobile** Series 88 Futuramic Sedan was in Olds' medium range. It was very similar to the Series 76 but the engine was a 303·7 CID V8. Top-line models were in Series 98. These had the same V8 engine but 122-in wb and larger body. All models could be ordered with Hydra-Matic Drive and most were. Total 1950 production was 396,757 cars, including the three-millionth since 1897.

8B: **Oldsmobile** Series 88 Futuramic DeLuxe Holiday Coupé. This Fisher hardtop body was also used by Chevrolet (Bel Air) and Pontiac (Catalina). Wb 119½ in.

8C: **Packard** produced their 23rd Series from May 1949 until the summer of 1950. There were various wheelbase sizes, 8-cyl. in-line engines and body styles. Some had Ultramatic automatic transmission. In addition there were an export-only Six on 120-in wb and a New York type taxicab with the same 245 CID engine but on 141-in wb.

Shown is a DeLuxe Super Eight Sedan with 127-in wb and 327 CID engine.

8D: **Plymouth** offered various body styles in three series: P-19 DeLuxe with 111-in wb and P-20 DeLuxe and P-20 Special DeLuxe (shown), both with 118½-in wb. DeSoto and Dodge dealers in certain export territories sold the same car with distinguishing radiator grilles as Diplomat and Kingsway respectively. All had 217·8 CID 97-bhp L-head Six engine and were similar in most respects to 1949 production.

8E: **Pontiac** Silver Streak Chieftain four-door Sedan was available in both the Series 25 Six (239·2 CID) and the Series 27 Eight (268·4 CID). Engines were in-line L-heads. Of Coupés and Sedans there were fastback versions named Streamliner. New this year was the Catalina Hardtop Coupé. Wheelbase of all models was 120 in and Hydra-Matic Drive was optional.

8A Oldsmobile 88

8C Packard DeLuxe Super Eight

8D Plymouth Special DeLuxe

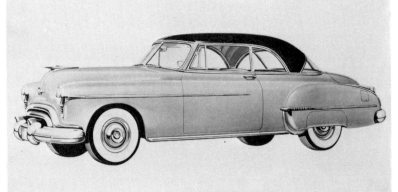

8B Oldsmobile 88

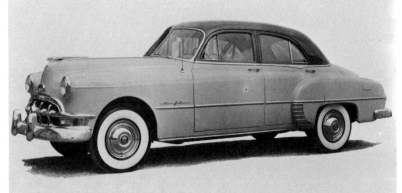

8E Pontiac Chieftain

9A : **Studebaker** 1950 models had restyled front end and new coil spring front suspension, replacing transversal leaf type. Shown is the Model 9G-Q1 Champion DeLuxe 3-pass. Coupé which had 113-in wb and 85-bhp 169·6 CID L-head Six engine. Five-pass. Coupés, two- and four-door Sedans and a Convertible were also available.

9B : **Studebaker** Commander Land Cruiser, Model 17A-Y5, was top-line sedan. Mechanically similar to other Commanders, its wheelbase was four inches longer, at 124 in. The engine was a 102-bhp 245·6 CID L-head Six. All Champion body styles were available also on the 120-in wb Commander chassis.

9C : **Willys** produced the famed Universal Jeep, CJ3A, as well as a wide range of Jeep-inspired models including Jeepster Phaetons, Station Wagons and Pickups. Some types were available with either conventional (4 × 2) or all-wheel drive (4 × 4). For use in the Korean conflict, the US Army ordered a military version of the CJ3A and a substantial number of these (designated Truck, ¼-ton, 4 × 4, Utility, M38) were built during 1950–52. One of these is shown.

9D : **Willys** Jeepster Phaeton, styled by Brooks Stevens, was first introduced in May 1948. In 1950 it was available with either the 134 CID Four or 161 CID Six engine. Wb was 104 in.

9C Willys Jeep

9A Studebaker Champion

9B Studebaker Land Cruiser

9D Willys Jeepster

1951

In spite of government restrictions, the US automotive industry in 1951 sold 5,338,435 new cars, including the 100-millionth. Most models were 'carry-overs' from 1950 with the customary annual facelifts. Only Kaiser-Frazer's and Packard's 1951 models were entirely new. Ford and Plymouth introduced their first hardtops, the Victoria and Belvedere respectively. Hardtops, which became very fashionable, resembled convertible coupés except that the tops were made of metal and could not be folded down.

Cadillac began producing Walker Bulldog tanks in their Cleveland, Ohio, Ordnance plant and Ford started design work on a new field car, the $\frac{1}{4}$-ton 4×4 military Utility Truck, XM151. At the other extreme, a new 'dream car' campaign, which was to continue throughout the 1950s, commenced with Chrysler displaying their K370 experimental car and General Motors their LeSabre and Buick XP300. The latter had a supercharged 300-bhp V8 power plant. Although most of these dream cars were genuine test beds for new ideas and developments and were exhibited to gauge the public's reaction to advanced styling concepts, others were probably made chiefly to impress and 'get in on the act'.

10B Buick Super

10A Buick Special

10C Cadillac 62

10A : **Buick** Series 40 Special Convertible, Model 46C. 1951 Buick model range comprised six Series 40 Special models, eight Series 50 Supers and six Series 70 Roadmasters.

10B : **Buick** Series 50 Super, Model 56R Riviera Hardtop. Special and Super models now had the same 263 CID ($3\frac{3}{16} \times 4\frac{1}{8}$-in) engine ; the Roadmasters had the larger 320 CID ($3\frac{7}{16} \times 4\frac{5}{16}$-in) power unit as before. All were in-line OHV Eights.

10C : **Cadillac** Series 62 Sedan, Model 6219. 1951 models were not much different from 1950, but the lowest-priced Series 61 was dropped.

10D : **Cadillac** Series 86 long-wheelbase (163-in) commercial chassis with ambulance bodywork by Superior, for US Army.

10D Cadillac 86/Superior

11A Checker Cab

11B Chevrolet Styleline DeLuxe

11C Chrysler New Yorker

11D DeSoto Custom

11A: **Checker** produced large numbers of purpose-designed taxicabs. Shown is a typical standard model of the early 1950s. Note sturdy bumpers and overriders and location of rear axle, set well back for easy entrance and maximum interior space.

11B: **Chevrolet** Series 2100JK Styleline DeLuxe four-door Sedan, Model 2103. Other models in this series: two-door Sedan, Station Wagon (steel), Sport Coupé, Convertible Coupé and Bel Air Coupé (hardtop). Both Sedans were available with fastback also.

11C: **Chrysler** offered two Sixes (Windsor C-51-1 and Windsor DeLuxe C-51-2) and two V8s (New Yorker C-52 and Saratoga C-55). Wheelbase was 125½ in for C-51 and C-55, 131½ in for C-52. The V8 was Chrysler's first. It was a 331·1 CID OHV unit with hemispherical combustion chambers. Named FirePower, it became known popularly as the Chrysler 'Hemi'. Its original output was 180 bhp. The 116-bhp 250·6 CID Six was later superseded by a longer-stroke 264·5 CID engine with 119-bhp rating. In addition to the above there were 131½- and 145½-in wb Imperial V8s (see 1952). Illustrated: New Yorker Sedan.

11D: **DeSoto** Custom Sedan featured revised front end styling. Engine piston stroke was increased, resulting in greater piston displacement (250·6 vs. 236·7 cu.in). Power output was up from 112 to 116 bhp. Again there were DeLuxe (S-15-1) and Custom (S-15-2) series, both with 125½-in wb, as well as some special 139½-in models and the 118½-in wb Diplomat SP-23 (for export). Tip-Toe hydraulic shift with Gyrol Fluid Drive was standard on Custom, optional on DeLuxe models (as in 1949–50).

1951

12A: **Dodge** offered three L-head Six ranges: D-40 Kingsway (export only), D-41 Wayfarer (115-in wb) and D-42 Meadowbrook and Coronet (123½-in wb). An exception in the latter series was an 8-seat sedan which had 137½-in wb. Bodywork was similar to 1950 except for restyled front end. Shown is a Coronet Sedan.

12B: **Ford** range comprised Six (1HA) and V8 (1BA) models with DeLuxe and Custom versions for Coupés, Tudors and Fordors. Station wagons were offered only in the Custom lines, Convertibles and Victoria Hardtops only as Custom V8. All had 114-in wb. Illustrated: Series 1BA V8 Custom Fordor, Model 73B, available with conventional, overdrive or the new Fordomatic automatic transmission.

12C: **Ford** V8 Custom Country Squire Station Wagon, Model 79, was most expensive 1951 Ford, with a list price of $2022. It was also available with the 95-bhp flat-head Six engine, at $1945.

12D: **Frazer** 1951 models were introduced as early as March 31, 1950. The bodywork was completely restyled, by Howard A. Darrin. Five models were available: Series F515 four-door Sedan and Vagabond (utility) and Series F516 Manhattan four-door steel-top and nylon-covered steel-top Sedans and Convertible. Wheelbase was 123½ in, engine was, as before, the Continental 226·2 CID flat-head Six. This was the last year of the Frazer.

12E: **Hudson** 1951 A Series, consisted of Pacemaker Custom 4A, Super Six Custom 5A, Commodore Six Custom 6A, Hornet 7A and Commodore Eight Custom 8A models. The Hornet (shown) had a 308 CID Six engine and 124-in wb; other models had engines and wheelbases as in 1950. A new Hardtop model, the Hollywood, was available from Sept. 1951 in all series except Pacemaker. Hydra-Matic automatic transmission was optional.

12A Dodge Coronet

12C Ford V8 Country Squire

12D Frazer

12B Ford V8 Custom

12E Hudson Hornet

13A Kaiser DeLuxe

13B Kaiser Henry J

13C Lincoln

13A: **Kaiser** announced completely new 1951 models in May 1950. Like the preceding design they were styled by Howard A. Darrin and very good looking. There were two ranges, Special K511 and DeLuxe K512, each with two- and four-door Sedans and Travelers, and Coupés. All had 118½-in wb and Continental 226·2 CID 115-bhp flat-head Sixes. Conventional, overdrive and automatic (GM Hydra-Matic) transmission were available. Shown : DeLuxe four-door Sedan.

13B: **Kaiser** introduced a small 100-in wb two-door sedan in September, 1950. Announced as the all-new Low Priced Car it was soon given a marque name : Henry J, after Kaiser-Frazer's president Henry J. Kaiser. There were two versions : Standard K513 with 134·2 CID Four and DeLuxe K514 with 161 CID Six. Engines were supplied by Willys.

13C: **Lincoln** produced two lines : 1EL Coupé, Lido Coupé and Sport Sedan and 1EH Cosmopolitan Coupé, Capri Coupé, Convertible and Sport Sedan. Shown is the Model 1EL-74 Sport Sedan.

13D: **Mercury** featured various minor styling changes and a larger rear window. New Merc-O-Matic auto. trans. was optional. Output of the 225·4 CID V8 was increased to 112 bhp. Shown : Model 1M-72 Coupé.

13E: **Mercury** Convertible, Model 1M-76, with rear wheel shields.

13D Mercury

13E Mercury

1951

14A: **Meteor**, produced by Ford of Canada, resembled US Ford in most respects.

14B: **Nash** model availability for 1951 was extended with a third and a fourth Rambler, namely a Super Suburban and a Custom Hardtop (from June). Statesman and Ambassador models had new grilles and restyled wings, as exemplified by this Ambassador Custom two-door Sedan.

14C: **Oldsmobile** dropped the Six and for 1951 offered only V8 engines. Known as Rocket, these OHV high-compression power units had first been introduced in 1948. The former 6-cylinder engine plant was converted for production of bazooka rockets. The Super 88 (shown) was new for 1951 and had leaf springs at the rear instead of coil springs as on 88. 88 and Super 88 models had 119½- and 120-in wb respectively.

14D: **Oldsmobile** Series 98 Holiday Sedan was one of four models in Olds' top-line. Engine was 303·7 CID Rocket V8, wheelbase 122 in. Hydra-Matic drive was optional on all Oldsmobiles.

14E: **Packard** had new bodywork for the 24th Series, which went into production on 21 August 1950. There were four series, all with eight-in-line L-head engines, viz: 200 with 122-in wb and 288 CID engine, 250 with same wb but 327 CID engine, 300 (shown) with engine as 250 but 127-in wb, and Patrician 400 with engine and wb as 300 but with Ultramatic transmission as standard (optional on others). Station wagons were discontinued.

14A Meteor

14D Oldsmobile Ninety-Eight

14B Nash Ambassador

14C Oldsmobile Super 88

14E Packard 300

15A: **Plymouth** P-23 Cranbrook (Sedan illustrated) and Cambridge had 118½-in wb. The third model range was the P-22 Concord with 111-in wb. All had a 217·8 CID (3¼ × 4⅜ in) side-valve Six and were in production until September 1952.

15B: **Pontiac** 1951 Silver Anniversary models were much the same as the 1950 range. Body style availability was also the same except that the Streamliner four-door fastback Sedans were dropped. The L-head Six and Eight power units developed 96 and 116 bhp respectively. Wheelbase was 120 in. Illustrated : Silver Streak Chieftain Six DeLuxe Convertible Coupé.

15C: **Studebaker** Commander Regal 5-pass. Coupé, Model H-C3. 1951 models had revised grille but otherwise were much like the 1947–50 models. Wheelbase of the Commanders was 115 in (except Land Cruiser, 119) and they were powered by a new OHV V8 engine of 232·6 CID ; Champion models (now with 115-in wb) retained the 169·6 CID flat-head Six. Overdrive and auto.trans. were optional.

15D: **Willys** continued the 80-in wb Universal Jeep, CJ3A, which retained the war-proven 134 CID L-head Four engine, and its range of 104-in wb Jeepsters, Station Wagons and light trucks. A 161 CID L-head Six engine was optionally available in Jeepsters and Station Wagons.

15A Plymouth Cranbrook

15B Pontiac Chieftain Six

15C Studebaker Commander

15D Willys 473 Station Wagon

1952

In 1952 Studebaker celebrated their 100th anniversary, Cadillac and the AAA (American Automobile Association) their 50th. Willys produced their 1,100,000th utility-type vehicle, a civilian Universal Jeep, since they built their first military Jeep—just over 10 years earlier. Chevrolet produced their 1-millionth Powerglide automatic transmission. Charles E. Wilson, president of General Motors, was named Secretary of Defense in the Eisenhower Cabinet and Harlow H. Curtice succeeded him as GM president. Many automotive firms were engaged in defence production, including aircraft engines (Buick, Kaiser-Frazer, Studebaker), tanks, guns and other munitions. In addition they sold 4,320,794 cars and almost 1¼ million trucks and buses. Powel Crosley retired as president-treasurer of Crosley Motors after General Tire and Rubber bought the company. Production of the little Crosley cars, first introduced in 1939, was discontinued in July. Henry Ford's Dearborn Motors Corp. settled suit with Henry Ferguson for 9¼ million dollars, ending the Ford Dearborn/Ferguson tractor patents litigation. Many 1952 cars featured a one-piece windscreen.

16A Buick Special

16A: **Buick** 1952 range did not differ much from the preceding model year. Again there were three series: 40 Special (6 models), 50 Super (5) and 70 Roadmaster (5). The latter had, as usual, four 'port-holes' as against three on the others. Illustrated is the Series 40 Special, Model 41D, which had a 263 CID 8-in-line engine and 121½-in wb.

16B: **Buick** Series 50 Super Convertible, Model 56C.

16C: **Cadillac** Series 62 Sedan, Model 6219. Series 60 75 were also available as previously. The engine was an improved 190-bhp high-compression OHV V8 with four-barrel carburettor. The Hydra-Matic transmission (optional on Series 75, standard on others) now had three forward ranges viz: *Drive*, first position (D1) for all four gear ratios, second (D2) for up to third ratio, *Low* (L) for up to second ratio. A new power steering system was also introduced.

16B Buick Super

16C Cadillac 62

17A Chevrolet Styleline DeLuxe

17B Chevrolet Styleline DeLuxe

17C Chrysler Windsor

17D Chrysler Imperial

17A : **Chevrolet** Series 2100KK Styleline DeLuxe Sedan, Model 2103.
1952 models were the last facelifted editions of the models which were
introduced in 1949. Body style availability was much the same as in
1949 except that during 1950–51 the Bel Air Hardtop Coupé had been
added and the fastback four-door Fleetline Sedans and the Station
Wagon with wooden body had been dropped.
17B : **Chevrolet** Series 2100KK Styleline DeLuxe Convertible, Model
2134. Convertibles with Powerglide transmission had 7·10-15 tyres,
instead of 6·70-15 as on all other models.
17C : **Chrysler** 1952 models were similar to 1951 except for revised
tail lamps. Shown is the 125½-in wb Windsor C-51 four-door Sedan.
17D : **Chrysler** Imperial C-54 had same wheelbase as the Chrysler
New Yorker (131½-in). The C-53 Crown Imperial had the longer
145½-in wb chassis, as previous Imperials, and was offered as
8-passenger Sedan and Limousine with PAS as standard equipment.
Both series had the Chrysler 331·1 CID 180-bhp 'hemi-head' V8.

1952

18A: **DeSoto** DeLuxe S-15-1 and Custom S-15-2 were much the same as before. New in 1952 was the Firedome, Series S-17, which featured a 276·1 CID 160-bhp version of Chrysler's new 'hemi-head' eight-cylinder-in-Vee engine. Shown is the Firedome Hardtop Coupé.

18B: **DeSoto** Series SP-23 Diplomat was, in effect, 118½-in wb Plymouth with distinguishing trimmings, providing DeSoto dealers in certain overseas territories such as W. Europe and Australia with a lower-price car.

18C: **Dodge** 1952 model range was the same as in 1951, with the exception of the Sportabout in the D-41 Wayfarer line which was

discontinued (it had been introduced in 1949 as Dodge's post-war roadster). New on 1951/52 models were Oriflow shock absorbers and instrument panels with leather-grained finish to reduce glare.

18D: **Ford** offered three lines: Mainline, Customline and Crestline. The bodywork was restyled and now featured a one-piece windscreen. The Courier Sedan Delivery and Ranch Wagon 2-door Station Wagon were similar to the Mainline, except for the rear body. The Country Squire 4-door Station Wagon, Victoria Hardtop and Sunliner Convertible were in the Crestline series. Six-cylinder engines now had overhead valves. Shown: Customline Country Sedan, Model 79B.

18C Dodge Coronet

18A DeSoto Firedome

18B DeSoto Diplomat

18D Ford Country Sedan

19A: **Ford** Crestline V8 Victoria, Model 60B. Sunliner was Convertible variant. These top-line models sold at $2105 and $2215 resp. Intermediate Customline models had same body side mouldings.

19B: **Henry J** Corsair was Kaiser-Frazer's small two-door Sedan with 100-in wb. The K523 standard model had a 4-cyl. 68-bhp 134·2 CID engine. The K524 DeLuxe had bumper overriders and a 6-cyl. 80-bhp 161 CID engine. Both power units were Willys-made L-heads. A special version, named Allstate, was launched by Sears, Roebuck & Co. It had a slightly different grille with two horizontal bars and separately mounted side lights. For 1951 Henry J see Kaiser 1951 (13B).

19C: **Hudson** 1952 B Series consisted of five model ranges:

Pacemaker 4B, Wasp 5B, Commodore Six 6B, Hornet 7B and Commodore Eight 8B. Pacemakers and Wasps had 119-in, the others 124-in wb. All had six-cylinder engines, except the Commodore Eight, of which the Convertible model is illustrated. The Wasp was a new low-priced line.

19D: **Kaiser** Manhattan four-door Sedan was Kaiser-Frazer's top-line model. Except for one-piece windscreen and some styling changes to the front end, the car was similar to last year's DeLuxe. The DeLuxe name was now employed for what used to be the Special. The higher-priced Frazer line was discontinued and the small Kaiser was sold under the Henry J marque name (*q.v.*).

19A Ford Crestline

19B Henry J Corsair

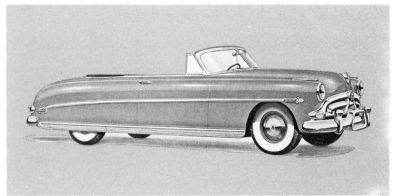

19C Hudson Commodore Eight

19D Kaiser Manhattan

1952

20A Lincoln Capri

20B Mercury

20C Meteor Customline

20A : **Lincoln** had entirely new bodywork and showed more family resemblance to the Ford and Mercury than before. Teamed up with the 160-bhp flat-head V8 was GM's successful Hydra-Matic (the fitting of which was by no means confined to General Motors products). Shown is the smartly styled Capri Special Custom Hard Top Coupé.

20B : **Mercury** Sport Coupé, Model MA-60E. MA Series had all new bodywork. The V8 engine was uprated to 125 bhp and there were eight bodystyles : Monterey and Sport Coupés (60B and E), two-door Sedan (70B), four-door Sedan and Monterey Sedan (73B and C), Monterey Convertible (76B), eight- and six-pass. Station Wagons (79B and D). Conventional, overdrive and automatic transmissions were available.

20C : **Meteor** Customline V8 Fordor, produced by Ford of Canada.

20D : **Nash** Rambler Custom Greenbrier Station Wagon, Model 5224, was available with two-tone paint finish. Wheelbase was 100 in, engine L-head Six.

20E : **Nash** Statesman and Ambassador models featured entirely new styling with Airflyte unitary body-cum-chassis construction. Wheelbase was $114\frac{1}{4}$ and $121\frac{1}{4}$ in resp. Shown is an Ambassador Country Club Hardtop, Model 5277.

20D Nash Rambler

20E Nash Ambassador

21A: **Oldsmobile** DeLuxe 88 was available as two- or four-door Sedan. This lowest-priced range now had the same larger Fisher body as the Super 88 and the same 120-in wb. The Rocket V8 had a two-barrel carb. and was rated at 145 bhp.

21B: **Oldsmobile** Super 88 was more luxurious version of DeLuxe 88 and had same engine as the top-line 98 (160-bhp with four-barrel Quadri-Jet carb.).

21C: **Oldsmobile** 98 Holiday Coupé. All 98s had new body styling. Olds introduced optional PAS, dual-range Hydra-Matic Super Drive and the Autronic-Eye, an automatic headlight dimmer.

21D: **Packard** 25th Series Patrician 400 Sedan was company's top-line model and featured further refined Ultramatic Drive auto.trans. as standard. New Easamatic vacuum power brakes, reducing pedal pressure by 40 per cent, were an optional extra. Body styling was substantially the same as in 1951. During 1951–52 an Ambulance and a Hearse were available in the 300 Series.

21B Oldsmobile Super 88

21C Oldsmobile Ninety-Eight

21A Oldsmobile DeLuxe 88

21D Packard Patrician 400

1952

BEAUTY AND FUNCTION. The Plymouth, like all Chrysler Corporation cars, is styled not by body designers alone, but by engineers, production men and designers working together. From the finely-appointed interior to gleaming finish, it is designed and engineered to give superlative transportation.

BEAUTY AND SPACE. Wide seats, and ample head room in this De Soto. Extra space inside, no extra bulk outside.

WHAT'S THE BEAUTY SECRET OF CHRYSLER-BUILT CARS?

A car need not be four wheels, a body and an engine lumped into any shape that designers please. It can be a graceful mechanism, the form of which is chiefly determined by function.

This is the practical principle that underlies the building of every Plymouth, Dodge, De Soto and Chrysler.

A plain example is the beautiful flowing lines of the roof on a Chrysler-built car. Chrysler engineers and designers consider the passengers' needs—the space for sitting, the depth of seats, the clearance between head and roof. All this is function. The graceful outer form follows.

This approach to design produces cars which are rightly proportioned, handsome, and eminently suited to your purposes.

CHRYSLER CORPORATION engineers and builds
PLYMOUTH, DODGE, DE SOTO, CHRYSLER CARS & DODGE TRUCKS
Chrysler Marine & Industrial Engines • Oilite Powdered Metal Products • Mopar Parts & Accessories • Airtemp Heating, Air Conditioning, Refrigeration • Cycleweld Cement Products

BEAUTY AND VISIBILITY. Note how much glass area this Chrysler has all around. Visibility blends with beauty, too.

BEAUTY AND COMFORT. Seats in this Dodge, as in all Chrysler-built cars, are chair height. And the whole interior is harmoniously and fashionably designed.

22A Plymouth Cranbrook

22B Pontiac Chieftain

22C Studebaker Champion

22A: **Plymouth** 1952 models were 'carry-overs' from 1951 and continued until entirely new models were introduced in October. The Cranbrook Belvedere, shown here heading a September 1952 Chrysler Corp. advertisement, was Plymouth's first Hardtop.

22B: **Pontiac** 1952 models looked identical to 1951 with the exception of the body side mouldings. The fastback Streamliner models were now discontinued altogether. Technically, however, there were further-reaching changes, namely availability of new power trains consisting of high-compression engines and new dual-range Hydra-Matic Drive. This new transmission was an optional extra with the high-compression engines.

22D Willys Aero-Ace

22C: **Studebaker** started their second century as vehicle manufacturers with the production of this Model 12G-W5 Champion Regal Sedan at South Bend, Indiana, on 18 Feb. 1952. It was 100 years and two days after the Studebaker brothers opened their wagon-building and blacksmith shop. In its first century Studebaker turned out over seven million horse-drawn and motor vehicles. Mechanically the 1952 cars were similar to 1951.

22D: **Willys** offered their first post-war passenger cars, the Aero-Ace and the Aero-Wing. They were of compact unit-welded body/chassis construction with a new 90-bhp Hurricane F-head (inlet-over-exhaust) six-cylinder 161 CID engine. Shown is the Aero-Ace, which had a wider rear window and more luxurious trim than the Aero-Wing.

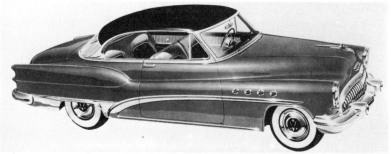

23A Buick Roadmaster

23B Buick Skylark

23C Cadillac El Dorado

1953

More 'dream cars' appeared during 1953: Buick's Wildcat, Dodge's Firearrow, Hudson's Italia, Lincoln-Mercury's XL500 and Packard's Balboa. A 'dream car come true' was Chevrolet's plastic-bodied Corvette. It became one of the most successful American sports cars.

A total of 6,116,948 cars were sold in the US in 1953, and the majority of these had eight-cylinder engines, many of them being V8s. Most car makers now offered automatic transmission and several top-line models featured it as standard equipment. Buick and Ford celebrated their golden anniversaries and in April Willys-Overland was purchased by the Kaiser Motors Corporation (formerly Kaiser-Frazer Corp.). Kaiser's Willow Run plant, built originally by Ford in 1942 for bomber production, was sold to General Motors for manufacture of Hydra-Matic transmissions, following the multi-million-dollar fire which destroyed their transmission plant at Livonia, also in Michigan. As a temporary measure, Cadillac and Oldsmobile buyers were offered Buick's Dynaflow and Pontiac adapted Chevrolet's Powerglide for their automatic transmission cars.

23A: **Buick** Roadmaster Riviera Hardtop, Model 76R. 1953 models had minor styling changes. Super 50 and Roadmaster 70 models had a new OHV V8 engine with bore and stroke of $4 \times 3 \cdot 2$ in. The Special 40 Series retained the $3\frac{3}{16} \times 4\frac{1}{8}$-in eight-in-line.

23B: **Buick** offered a new luxury convertible in the $5000 price bracket. Called Skylark it was based on the Roadmaster but did not have the customary 'port-holes'.

23C: **Cadillac** El Dorado Convertible was luxurious new model with panoramic windscreen and an overall height of $58\frac{1}{2}$ in. Interior was trimmed in leather. Cadillac offered the most powerful engine (210 bhp) ever used in an American production car.

1953

24A Checker Cab

24B Chevrolet Bel Air

24C Chevrolet Corvette

24D Chrysler New Yorker

24A: **Checker** taxicab styling had not changed much since about 1948 and continued until 1955/56. Checkers were also available as family cars but few were sold. The 'big three' offered taxicab versions of their popular models, mainly Chevrolet, Ford and DeSoto. Large numbers of these saw service throughout the United States and elsewhere.

24B: **Chevrolet** Series 2400 Bel Air Sedan, Model 2403. Fisher bodywork for 1953 Chevrolet was completely new. There were three series: One-Fifty or 1500 Special, Two-Ten or 2100 DeLuxe and 2400 Bel Air, with 6, 7 and 4 body styles respectively. Manual transmission cars had 235 CID 108-bhp engine (1952 Powerglide engine with hyd. valve lifters). Powerglide-equipped cars had new

115-bhp Blue-Flame, featuring aluminium pistons, insert connecting rod bearings and full pressure lubrication. All had one-piece windscreen.

24C: **Chevrolet** Corvette plastic-bodied Sport Roadster made its debut this year. It had a 150-bhp six-cylinder Blue-Flame engine and Powerglide transmission. In later years it was available with a wide range of engine performance options.

24D: **Chrysler** New Yorker Sedan. Chrysler dropped the Saratoga and offered C-60-1 Windsor and C-60-2 Windsor DeLuxe models with 264·5 CID 119-bhp Six and C-56-1 New Yorker and C-56-2 New Yorker DeLuxe with 331·5 CID 180-bhp V8. All had 125½-in wb. From June, PowerFlite was available. This was Chrysler's first full automatic.

25A Chrysler Imperial

25C DeSoto Diplomat Custom

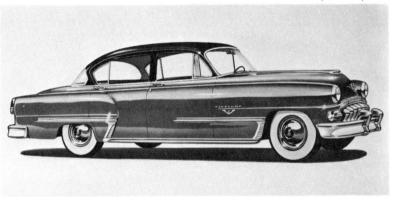

25B DeSoto Firedome

25D Dodge Coronet

25A: **Chrysler** Imperial series comprised luxurious C-58 Custom Imperial with 133½-in wb (shown) and C-59 Crown Imperial with 145½-in wb. Both had the same 180-bhp 'hemi-head' engine as regular Chryslers. The new PowerFlite auto.trans. was installed on Imperials beginning in March. The C-59 had 12-volt electrics.

25B: **DeSoto** Firedome V8 Sedan. Models with six-cylinder engine were redesignated Powermaster (Series S-18), the V8 retained the Firedome name (Series S-16). The two engines were rated at 116 and 160 bhp resp. Wheelbase was 125½-in for all regular models. Firedome Eight models outsold the Powermaster Six by almost two-to-one. Firedome was sometimes written as FireDome.

25C: **DeSoto** SP-24 Diplomat and Diplomat Custom (shown) were available for export with nine body styles. Like the Dodge Kingsway these 114-in wb economy models were mechanically similar to the Plymouth (q.v.) but they had 7·0:1 CR engines, rated at 97 bhp, like 1949–52 Plymouth.

25D: **Dodge** introduced its first V8. Named Red Ram and featuring hemispherical combustion chambers, it was a 241·3 CID unit, rated at 140 bhp. Over half the Dodges sold this year were V8s. 1953 series comprised Kingsway (export), D-46 Meadowbrook and Coronet Six with 119-in wb, D-47 Meadowbrook Six with 114-in wb, D-44 Coronet V8 with 119-in wb and D-48 Coronet V8 with 114-in wb (illustrated).

1953

26A: **Ford** 1953 range was virtually the same as that of 1952, in spite of the fact that this was Ford's 50th anniversary. The usual annual styling changes were confined mainly to the radiator grille and body side mouldings. Shown is the top-line Victoria Convertible, Model 60B, of the Crestline series.

26B: **Henry J** 1953 had same appearance as 1952 model but featured many detail improvements. There were Corsair-4 and Corsair DeLuxe (6-cyl.) versions. Sales literature listed 'Penny-Minder' carburettor, 'Synchro-Flex' rear springing, 'Triple-Tooth' steering with 'Finger-Tip' linkage, etc. However, this little Kaiser was discontinued after Kaiser bought Willys-Overland who had their Aero compact cars.

26C: **Hudson** C Series comprised Jet 1C and Super Jet 2C with 105-in wb, Wasp 4C and Super Wasp 5C with 119-in wb, and Hornet 7C with 124-in wb. All had Six in-line engines. The new Jet and Super Jet (shown) had a 104-bhp 3·3-litre engine, with 114-bhp twin-carb option and were available with conventional, overdrive or automatic (GM Hydra-Matic) transmission.

26D: **Kaiser** had won international beauty prizes during 1950–52 in France, Holland, Switzerland, etc. and for 1953 the DeLuxe and Manhattan models were continued with only minor changes. Coupé and Traveler models were discontinued. Illustrated is the DeLuxe four-door Sedan.

26B Henry J Corsair

26C Hudson Super Jet

26A Ford Crestline

26D Kaiser DeLuxe

27A: Lincoln Cosmopolitan Hardtop Coupé. 1953 styling changes were slight. Big news was under the bonnet (hood): a brand-new 317·5 CID OHV V8 with four-barrel concentric-bowl carburettor, developing 205 bhp at 4200 rpm. Transmission was dual-range Hydra-Matic (later Turbo-Drive) and 'power' was available for steering, braking and seat adjustment. There were three Capri and two Cosmopolitan models.

27B: Mercury 1953 MA Series was similar to 1952 except for minor styling changes. Model availability was also the same, except that the six-passenger station wagon was discontinued.

27C: Meteor, produced by Ford of Canada, differed from US Ford in grille and brightwork details.

27D: Nash 1953 range comprised four Rambler (Convertible shown), five Statesman and five Ambassador models. Ramblers equipped with Hydra-Matic had the same bore and stroke as the larger Statesman ($3\frac{1}{8} \times 4\frac{1}{4}$ in vs. $3\frac{1}{8} \times 4$ on other Ramblers).

27E: Nash-Healey Le Mans Hardtop Coupé was additional to the already existing Convertible/Roadster. Chassis came from Donald Healey in Warwick, England (using twin-carb. 140-bhp Nash Dual Jetfire Six engines), bodies from Pininfarina in Italy. Altogether 506 were made until August 1954.

27B Mercury

27C Meteor

27D Nash Rambler

27A Lincoln Cosmopolitan

27E Nash-Healey Le Mans

1953

28A: **Oldsmobile** Super 88 Holiday Coupé featured fashionable hardtop styling. Compared with 1952, 1953 models had squarer rear wings (fenders) and restyled grille, bumpers and side mouldings on otherwise unchanged Fisher bodies. This year's output of 319,414 cars included the company's four-millionth and the two-millionth with Hydra-Matic.

28B: **Oldsmobile** 98 Fiesta Convertible Coupé. Series 98 had 124-in wb, DeLuxe 88 and Super 88 120-in. All had 303 CID Rocket V8 engine, 165-bhp for 98 and Super 88, 150-bhp for DeLuxe 88, and 12-volt electrics.

28C: **Packard** 26th Series Patrician 400 six-passenger Sedan featured new body side mouldings, radiator grille and other detail changes. Eight-passenger and Limousine variants were introduced, as well as an attractive new sports roadster, called the Pan American. The latter had a 185-bhp eight-in-line engine and a top speed of 125 mph. In addition there were the 300 (three models), the Clipper range with a smaller-bore engine, and various Ambulances.

28D: **Plymouth** Cranbrook two-door Sedan. Range was simplified and now consisted of 114-in wb P-24-1 Cambridge and P-24-2 Cranbrook models. 217·8 CID engine was same as before but CR was increased from 7·0 to 7·1 :1, and output from 97 to 100 bhp, both at 3600 rpm. Hy-Drive auto.trans. was available for the first time.

28A Oldsmobile Super 88

28B Oldsmobile Ninety-Eight

28C Packard Patrician 400

28D Plymouth Cranbrook

29A: **Pontiac** Dual Streak 1953 range comprised Series 25 Chieftain Six and Series 27 Chieftain Eight, each with 11 models. Wheelbase was extended from 120 to 122 in. The engines used were still the in-line L-head 239·2 CID Six and 268·4 CID Eight. A number of Pontiacs were supplied with Powerglide auto.trans. (see p. 23).

29B: **Studebaker** introduced totally new body styling by Loewy, as exemplified by this Commander Regal Hardtop Coupé, Model 4H-K5. As usual there was a wide range of body styles in the Champion Series 14G and Commander Series 4H, topped by the luxurious Model 4H-Y5 Commander Regal Land Cruiser.

29C: **Willys** Aero-Ace Sedan. Aero range now comprised Lark, Falcon, Ace and Eagle two- and four-door models. Three engines were available: Lightning 6 (L-head, 75-bhp), Hurricane 4 (F-head, 72-bhp; Lark export option) and Hurricane 6 (F-head, 90-bhp).

29D: **Willys** CJ3B Universal Jeep was produced from 1952. It was basically the same as the preceding CJ3A but fitted with the new 71-bhp Hurricane 4 F-head engine, necessitating a higher hood (bonnet) and grille.

29E: **Willys** MD/M38A1 military Jeep was also produced from 1952. Mechanically similar to the CJ3B it had entirely new bodywork and 81-in (vs. 80-in) wb. For civilian use it was made available as CJ5 (see 37D).

29A Pontiac Chieftain

29C Willys Aero-Ace

29B Studebaker Commander

29D Willys Jeep

29E Willys Jeep

30A Buick Super

30B Buick Super

30C Cadillac

1954 This year saw important mergers involving four of the few remaining 'independents': Nash and Hudson formed the new American Motors Corporation and Studebaker and Packard combined into the Studebaker-Packard Corporation, both with headquarters in Detroit. Manufacturing was subsequently concentrated in Kenosha, Wisconsin and South Bend, Indiana, respectively. These two companies, together with the Kaiser-Willys combine, formed in the previous year, now battled against the 'big three' (General Motors, which produced its 50-millionth car, Ford and Chrysler), but only American Motors eventually stayed in business, after absorbing Kaiser-Willys (later Kaiser Jeep) in 1963.

Ford, following Chevrolet's lead in the two-seater sports-type car field, introduced its Thunderbird in October (see 1955). Experimental 'dream cars' this year included DeSoto's Adventurer II, Dodge's Granada, Ford's FX-Atmos, General Motors' gas turbine-powered Firebird XP21, Lincoln-Mercury's Monterey XM800, Packard's Panther and Plymouth's Belmont and Explorer.

Total passenger car sales reached just over 5½ million and by the end of the year tubeless tyres were being fitted on all new cars.

30D Cadillac 60 Special

30A: **Buick** reintroduced the Century range (Series 60), which had formerly been in existence during 1936–42. The other series were the 40 Special, 50 Super and 70 Roadmaster. Estate Wagons were available in the 40 and 60 Series, but dropped from the 50 and 70. Model availability numbered 16, including the Skylark Convertible, which was now designated M/100. All models had V8 engines. Wheelbase was 127 in on Series 50 and 70, 122 in on all others. Illustrated is the Series 50 Super Riviera, Model 52, with optional wire wheels.
30B: **Buick** Series 50 Super four-door Sedan, Model 52. All 1954 Buicks had panoramic windscreen.
30C: **Cadillac** were first to equip all their models with power steering. New grille was adapted from 1953 experimental LeMans fibreglass convertible.
30D: **Cadillac** Series 60 Special Fleetwood Sedan. All 1954 Cadillacs had wheelbase increased by three inches.

31A Chevrolet Two-Ten

31A : **Chevrolet** series 2100 (or Two-Ten) DeLuxe Sedan, Model 2103. Bodywork was much the same as for 1953, with styling changes mainly to radiator grille, bumpers and tail lights. Engines were Blue-Flame 115 for gearshift models, Blue-Flame 125 for models with Powerglide.

31B : **Chevrolet** period advertisement, showing series 2400 Bel Air Sport Coupé, model 2454.

31C : **Chrysler** programme was further reduced and now comprised Windsor DeLuxe C-62 Six, New Yorker and New Yorker DeLuxe C-63-1 and -2 V8. Body styles numbered six, five and four resp. The name Town & Country now applied to Station Wagons in Windsor DeLuxe and New Yorker lines. The Firepower 'hemi' engine developed 195 bhp in the C-63-1, 235 in the C-63-2. The Spitfire L-head Six of the C-62 was rated at 119 bhp. All had $125\frac{1}{2}$-in wb. Shown is a New Yorker Sedan.

31D : **Chrysler** Custom Imperial C-64 and Crown Imperial C-66 had $133\frac{1}{2}$- and $145\frac{1}{2}$-in wb resp. Both were powered by the 235-bhp version of Chrysler's Firepower V8.

31C Chrysler New Yorker

How the new Chevrolet wrings more **power** and more **miles** out of every gallon of gas...

31B Chevrolet Bel Air

31D Chrysler Imperial

1954

32A: DeSoto Powermaster Six S-20 and Firedome V8 S-19 retained the earlier wheelbase and engine dimensions, but CR and power output of the V8 were up from 7·1 to 7·5:1 and 160 to 170 bhp respectively. Sales of the V8 Firedome (shown) now accounted for 70% of total production. Chrysler's PowerFlite auto.trans. was made available as an optional extra.

32B: DeSoto Diplomat SP-25-1, Diplomat DeLuxe SP-25-2 and Diplomat Custom SP-25-3 were export models based on the Plymouth P-25-1, -2 and -3 resp. (q.v.). Engine was 217·8 CID (3·57-litre) 100-bhp with 7·1:1 CR. Hy-Drive auto.trans. was optional.

32C: Dodge Royal V8 Sedan. Dodge's US programme for 1954 was rather complex with eight basic series, two wheelbases and two engines: Sixes comprised D-51-1 Meadowbrook (wb 119 in), D-51-2 Coronet (119), and D-52 Coronet Suburban (114 or 119). These had the 230·2 CID 110-bhp 6-cyl. L-head engine. V8s comprised D-50-1

Meadowbrook, D-50-2 Coronet and D-50-3 Royal with 119-in wb, D-53-2 Coronet and D-53-3 Royal with 114-in wb. The 241·3 CID V8 provided 140 bhp in the Meadowbrook, 150 in all others. For export there was also the Plymouth-based Kingsway Series D-49 with 114-in wb.

32D: Ford used the same bodyshells as in 1953, albeit with styling changes to radiator grille and bright work. Illustrated are the Crestline Victoria Hardtop (Model/Body Type 60B) and the basic Mainline Tudor (70A). The former was also available, for the first time, with a transparent plastic roof front section. This model was called the Crestline Skyliner (60F). Other newcomers were the Crestline Fordor Sedan (73C) and Customline Ranch Wagon (59B). This year saw the end of the flat-head V8 engine in US production. It was superseded by a new 130-bhp OHV power unit. Every model could now be ordered with either the OHV Six or the new V8 engine.

32A DeSoto Firedome

32C Dodge Royal

32B DeSoto Diplomat

32D Ford Crestline and Mainline

33A : **Hudson** D Series consisted of Jet 1D, Super Jet 2D and Jet Liner 3D with 105-in wb, Wasp 4D and Super Wasp 5D with 119-in wb, and Hornet Special 6D and Hornet 7D models with 124-in wb, all with six-cylinder side-valve engines. This was the last year of 'real' Detroit-produced Hudsons. Only 32,293 were made. Illustrated is the Hornet Convertible Brougham.

33B : **Hudson** Jet four-door six-passenger Sedan. All Hudsons, except the Wasp, were optionally available with twin-carburettor (Twin H-Power) engine.

33C : **Kaiser** 1954 featured many detail changes, mainly to bumpers, radiator grille, tail lights, etc. The three-piece rear window was even larger than before. Low-priced models were named Special again and had the 226·2 CID Six which from 1953 was rated at 118 bhp. Manhattans had the same engine but were equipped with a supercharger, boosting the power output up to 140 bhp at 3900 rpm. Shown is the Manhattan four-door Sedan.

33D : **Kaiser-Darrin** 161. Kaiser-Willys, as the manufacturing organization was now known, also produced a fibreglass-bodied sports car, designed by Howard A. Darrin on the Kaiser chassis. It featured a three-position Deauville convertible top and sliding doors.

33A Hudson Hornet

33C Kaiser Manhattan

33B Hudson Jet

33D Kaiser-Darrin 161

1954

34A: **Lincoln** models were not much different from last year's.
Again there were Capri and Cosmopolitan models with various Coupé,
Convertible and Sedan body styles. Wheelbase and overall length were
123 and 215 inch resp. for all models. Shown is the Capri Special
Custom Convertible.

34B: **Mercury** Monterey Sun Valley Coupé featured transparent front
roof panel. A new 161-bhp overhead-valve V8 engine replaced the
earlier flat-head (side-valve) power unit on all models.

34C: **Meteor** standard Fordor V8, made by Ford of Canada.

34D: **Metropolitan** was a Nash-designed 85-in wb two-seater,
produced in Great Britain jointly by Austin and Fisher & Ludlow.
Hardtop and Convertible variants were available. First ten thousand cars
had 1200-cc engine (8/53-7/54), second series (8/54-7/55) had
1500-cc, both OHV. Nash sold the Metropolitan in the USA and
Canada.

34E: **Nash** Rambler Custom four-door Sedan, Model 5425, was new
and styled by Pininfarina. It had a 90-bhp L-head Six, known as Super
Flying Scot, and 108-in wb.

34C Meteor

34D Metropolitan

34A Lincoln Capri

34B Mercury Monterey

34E Nash Rambler

35A: **Nash** Rambler Custom Country Club Hardtop, Model 5427, had continental spare wheel mount as standard equipment and 100-in wb. Weather Eye air conditioning and radio were standard on the Super (Model 5417), optional on the Custom.

35B: **Nash** Ambassador Custom four-door Trunk Sedan, Model 5475, had 121¼-in wb and 130-bhp engine (OHV Six). Exterior spare wheel mount was standard on all Custom models in Statesman and Ambassador lines. Statesman had similar appearance but 114-in wb and 110-bhp Dual Powerflyte twin-carb. engine. All were styled by Pininfarina.

35C Oldsmobile Super 88

35A Nash Rambler

35D Oldsmobile Ninety-Eight

35B Nash Ambassador

35C: **Oldsmobile** Super 88 two-door Sedan. All 1954 models featured new body styling with panoramic windscreen and many technical detail changes and improvements. The V8 Rocket engine now developed 185 bhp.

35D: **Oldsmobile** 98 Deluxe Holiday Coupé. Production in 1954 reached 433,810 cars and Olds advanced to fourth place in US new car registrations during this year.

36A: **Packard** jumped from their 26th Series to the 54th and offered 212-bhp regular and 185-bhp Clipper ranges, each with seven body styles, not counting Ambulances and Hearses. New in the Clipper range was the Super Series which included a two-door Hardtop named Panama. The Convertible shown (from the regular range) featured Ultramatic No-Shift transmission which was now standard on most regular models and optional on others and Clipper models. Air-conditioning, PAS, PAB and tubeless tyres were optional also.

36B: **Plymouth** 1954 range comprised Plaza P-25-1, Savoy P-25-2 (Sedan shown) and Belvedere P-25-3 models, all on 114-in wb. Early production had same engine as 1953 but later the piston stroke was enlarged from $4\frac{3}{8}$ to $4\frac{5}{8}$ in, resulting in 230·2 (vs 217·8) CID. With

7·25 :1 CR the new engine developed 110 bhp and torque was increased from 177 to 190 lb ft at 1600 rpm. PAS and PowerFlite two-speed auto.trans. were optional.

36C: **Pontiac** introduced a new range of top-line cars, named Series 28 Star Chief Eight. It came in four variants: Convertible, Custom Catalina, DeLuxe Sedan and Custom Sedan (illustrated), all with 124-in wb. The 122-in wb Series 25 Chieftain Six and Series 27 Chieftain Eight were continued with nine models each. The Sedan Delivery was discontinued.

36D: **Pontiac** Star Chief Custom Catalina Hardtop Coupé, one of Pontiac's top-line models. In June this GM Division produced its five-millionth car (since 1926).

36A Packard

36C Pontiac Star Chief

36B Plymouth Savoy

36D Pontiac Star Chief

37A: **Studebaker** introduced its first Conestoga Station Wagons with DeLuxe and Regal versions in both the Champion (Series 15G) and Commander (Series 5H) ranges. Shown is the Commander V8 Regal Conestoga, Model 5H-D5, which, like the Champion version, had 116.5-in wb. Engine was 232.6 CID V8 (169.6 CID Six for Champion). Coupé models and Land Cruiser Sedan had 120.5-in wb, other Sedans 116.5.

37B: **Studebaker** Commander V8 Starliner Hardtop Coupé, Model 5H-K5. On 1 October Studebaker merged with Packard into the Studebaker-Packard Corporation, headquarted at Detroit (South Bend from 1956).

37C: **Willys** Aero-Eagle Custom Hardtop. Aero-Lark, -Ace and -Eagle models were now available with either the 161 CID Hurricane 6 90-bhp F-head engine or with the 115-bhp Continental 226.2 CID power unit which had been used in Kaiser and Frazer cars (*q.v.*). Willys called this the Super Hurricane, rather confusingly because unlike other Hurricanes it was an L-head (side-valve) engine. Conventional, Overdrive and Hydra-Matic transmissions were available.

37D: **Willys** offered two Universal Jeeps, the CJ3B (see 29D) and the more expensive CJ5 (shown) which was a 'de-militarized' Model MD ¼-ton 4×4 Utility Truck, M38A1 (see 29E). Both models had the 71-bhp Hurricane 4 engine and remained in production for many years, in North America and in overseas licencees' plants.

37A Studebaker Commander

37C Willys Aero-Eagle

37B Studebaker Commander

37D Willys Jeep

1955 During 1955 the automotive industry broke all records with a total production of 9,204,049 vehicles. Passenger car sales accounted for nearly eight million. Most manufacturers introduced entirely new cars for the 1955 model year, incorporating such features as panoramic windshields (wrap-around windscreens). Chevrolet, Packard, Pontiac and Plymouth offered OHV V8 engines. There was a host of new experimental cars from Buick (Wildcat III), Cadillac (Eldorado Brougham), Chevrolet (Biscayne), Chrysler (Flight Sweep), Ford (Mystere and Futura), General Motors

38B Buick Roadmaster

38A: **Buick** 1955 range comprised Series 40 Special, 50 Super, 60 Century and 70 Roadmaster models. Model availability per Series was six, three, five and three resp. All models now had four 'port-holes', except the Series 40 Special, which had three as before. Wheelbase was 122 in for Special and Century, 127 in for Super and Roadmaster. Sales were up almost 50% over 1954, at 738,152. Shown is the Series 60 Century Riviera Sedan, Model 63.
38B: **Buick** Series 70 Roadmaster Sedan, Model 72, combined new styling with 236-bhp V8 engine and new variable-pitch Dynaflow transmission.
38C: **Cadillac** Series 62 Sedan, Model 6219. With the main exception of front bumper and body side mouldings 1955 Cadillacs looked similar to the 1954 models.

38A Buick Century

(La Salle II with V6 engine and Firebird II with gas turbine), Oldsmobile (Delta) and Pontiac (Strato-Star).
    Kaiser Motors Corporation was reorganized as Kaiser Industries Corporation, with Willys Motors, Inc. a wholly-owned subsidiary. Both firms announced plans to discontinue passenger car production in the US and concentrate on the manufacture of civilian and military Jeep vehicles. During 1954–55 most car makers changed over from the traditional 6-volt to 12-volt electrical systems.

38C Cadillac 62

39A Cadillac 62

It's Making '55 Famous—For Fun!

For sheer driving pleasure, Chevrolet's stealing the thunder from the high-priced cars.

Let's be frank. Up to now, maybe there were reasons for wanting one of the higher priced cars. If you desired something really special in the way of driving fun, you simply had to pay a premium to get it. Usually, a big one!

Not any more! The Motoramic Chevrolet is taking the play away from the high-priced cars with pure excitement on wheels!

Chevrolet's new "Turbo-Fire V8" puts a

heaping hoodful of fun under your foot—162 h.p.! (Special to adventure lovers: 180 h.p. "Super Turbo-Fire V8" is optional at extra cost.) You can also choose from the two highest powered 6's in the low-price field.

As for drives, just name it. Chevrolet offers Overdrive, super-smooth Powerglide (extra-cost options) and a new and finer Synchro-Mesh transmission.

Find out how the Motoramic Chevrolet puts new fun-in your driving life! Take the key at your Chevrolet dealer's—and you'll want it for keeps! . . . Chevrolet Division of General Motors, Detroit 2, Michigan.

Motoramic **CHEVROLET**   *See and drive it at your Chevrolet dealer's*

39C Chevrolet Two-Ten

THE 100-MILLION-DOLLAR LOOK!

WINDSOR DELUXE NASSAU IN BRILLIANT TANGO RED AND PLATINUM

It's a totally new fashion in Tailored Steel

Now you see what all the excitement's about! Now you see the newest new car in this generation—the brilliantly different Chrysler for 1955 with its dramatically sweeping silhouette in tailored steel.

New longer, lower, leaner lines . . . luxurious new fashion-forecast interiors . . . new Super-Scenic Windshield with swept-back posts . . . new Twin-Tower tail lights that say "new" with great authority . . . new PowerFlite Range-Selector on the dash —new *everything* inside, new *everything* outside!

MORE NEWS: Every Chrysler is now a V-8 with engines up to 250 hp *Plus* PowerFlite, most automatic of all no-clutch transmissions . . . Full-Time Coaxial Power Steering, double-width pedal Power Brakes, Power Seats. And new tubeless tires!

See your Chrysler dealer as soon as you can and see why now, more than ever before, the power of leadership is yours in a Chrysler. You'll feel a new personal power and personal pride that the ordinary motorist cannot even imagine!

AMERICA'S MOST SMARTLY DIFFERENT CAR . . . **CHRYSLER** FOR 1955

39D Chrysler Windsor

39B Chevrolet Bel Air

39A: **Cadillac** Series 62 Coupé de Ville Celebrity, one of three specially appointed production show cars for GM's Motorama exhibition. An experimental car, Eldorado Brougham, was displayed also.

39B: **Chevrolet** Series 2400 Bel Air Sedan, Model 2403. All models were entirely new and an OHV V8 engine was available for most (previous Chevy V8 was in 1919). Other features included Hotchkiss drive rear axle, ball-jointed steering swivels, swing-type pedals, optional overdrive and air conditioning, etc.

39C: **Chevrolet** Series Two-Ten or 2100 DeLuxe Sedan, Model 2103. There was a choice of six engine/transmission combinations.

39D: **Chrysler** C-67 Windsor DeLuxe Nassau Hardtop featured a new 188-bhp 301 CID OHV V8 engine. The Six was dropped for good. All 1955 Chryslers had 126-in wb.

39E: **Chrysler** C-68 New Yorker DeLuxe Hardtop had improved 331 CID FirePower V8, rated at 250 bhp. Powerflite transmission (with range selector on dash), PAS and PAB were standard.

39E Chrysler New Yorker

1955

40A Chrysler 300

40B DeSoto Diplomat

40C DeSoto Fireflite

40A: **Chrysler** C-300, first of a new breed of Chrysler high-performance cars. It was named 300 since it was (at that time) 'the only stock car wielding 300 brute horsepower'.

40B: **DeSoto** SP-26 Diplomat and Diplomat Custom were technically similar to Plymouth Six Plaza and Belvedere respectively. There were also a Diplomat Six with 217·8 (vs 230) CID engine, designated SP-26X, and SP-27 V8s.

40C: **DeSoto** S-21 Fireflite was a new higher-priced addition to the line. It shared the 126-in wb chassis and 291 CID V8 engine with the S-22 Firedome but output differed (185 bhp for Firedome, 200 bhp for Fireflite). PAS and PAB were optional on both. The Six engine was discontinued for home market models.

40D: **DeSoto** Fireflite Sportsman Hardtop Coupé with two-tone paint.

40E: **Dodge** D-55-3 Custom Royal with 183-bhp Super Red Ram V8 engine. Other 1955 models included Kingsway Six (D-54, D-54X) and V8 (D-59), Coronet Six (D-56-1) and V8 (D-55-1), and Royal V8 (D-55-2). All except Kingsway (see Plymouth) had 120-in wb.

40D DeSoto Fireflite

40E Dodge Custom Royal

41A : **Ford** introduced entirely new models. The Crestline name was dropped for the top-line models and replaced by Fairlane. Shown is the Fairlane Fordor (73C). The basic Mainline and intermediate Customline had the same bodywork but less luxurious trim. All had $115\frac{1}{2}$-in wb and 272 CID V8 (Y-block) engine with 162 or 182 horsepower rating or the alternative 223 CID Six which now developed 120 bhp. Conventional, Overdrive and Fordomatic transmissions were available.

41B : **Ford** Fairlane Crown Victoria, Model 64A. On the Model 64B the front section of the roof was made of transparent plastic. Note tiara-like chrome strip arched over top of car.

41C : **Ford** Fairlane eight-pass. Country Squire, Model 79C. Ranch Wagons (59A, B) had two doors, Country Sedans (79B, D) four. For extra performance all V8-engined wagons had dual exhausts.

41D-E : **Ford** Thunderbird two-seater was beginning of a long line of 'T-birds', as they became popularly known. Engine was 292 CID Y-block V8, wb 102 in. There were convertible (Model 40A, shown) and hardtop (Model 40B) versions.

41C Ford Fairlane

41A Ford Fairlane

41D Ford Thunderbird

41B Ford Fairlane

41E Ford Thunderbird

1955

42A: **Hudson** production was transferred from Detroit to Kenosha, Wisconsin, as one of the results of the forming of the American Motors Corporation which took place in 1954, combining Nash and Hudson. 1955 Hudsons, were, in fact, variants of the Nash and Nash Rambler cars, with different front end and trim.

42B: **Imperial**, Chrysler's most luxurious line, was now a separate marque and, as before, competed with Ford's Lincoln and GM's Cadillac. The 1955 line consisted of C-69 Imperial and C-70 Crown Imperial (shown) models with 130- and 149½-in wb resp. Both had 250-bhp 331 CID V8.

42C: **Kaiser** was same as 1954 model and also last, at least in North America (see 67B). The company decided to concentrate on Jeep vehicles. Shown is a 1954/55 Kaiser Special two-door Sedan.

42D: **Kurtis** 500-M Sports Car was named after the Indianapolis 500-Mile Races where in 1954 cars designed and built by Frank Kurtis won all but seventh of the first ten places. The car was made by Kurtis Sports Car Corp. of Los Angeles, California and powered by a stock Cadillac V8 of 250 bhp. Top speed was 135 mph. A modified engine, good for 175+ mph, was optional.

42E: **Lincoln** Capri Coupé. 1952 type chassis and bodyshells were retained but many detail styling changes were made. Technical features included a new Turbo-Drive auto.trans. and improved larger-bore 341 CID 225-bhp V8 power plant with dual exhausts. A new air conditioning system and tubeless tyres were introduced also. There were standard and Capri models; the name Cosmopolitan was dropped.

42A Hudson Hornet

42D Kurtis 500-M

42B Imperial

42C Kaiser Special

42E Lincoln Capri

43A Mercury Montclair

43D Nash Statesman

43B Meteor Rideau

43E Oldsmobile Ninety-Eight

43C Nash Rambler

43A: **Mercury** introduced new models which were longer, wider and lower and featured 'full-scope' windscreen, new interior styling and more powerful engines (OHV V8, 188 and 198 bhp). In three series, Custom, Monterey and Montclair, there was a total of ten models. Illustrated is the top-line Montclair Coupé.

43B: **Meteor** Rideau four-door Sedan, a Ford-based Canadian product. Radiator grille featured heavy V-motif in centre.

43C: **Nash** Rambler model availability now numbered eight. They had a new grille and were also available as Hudson Rambler. Illustrated is the two-door Hardtop.

43D: **Nash** Statesman (shown) and Ambassador lines were reduced to four-door Sedans and two-door Hardtops. In addition to the OHV Six engine, a 208-bhp V8 with Ultramatic Drive was offered for the Ambassador. The Ultramatic auto.trans. was bought from Packard.

43E: **Oldsmobile** 1955 models featured new two-tone styling, redesigned front suspension and a 202-bhp Rocket engine. The first four-door Hardtop in the industry, the Holiday Sedan (98 DeLuxe shown), was introduced in March. Soon the Holiday two- and four-door hardtop models accounted for almost two-thirds of Olds' production. Super 88 models were similar in general appearance to 98 but had slightly shorter wheelbase.

44A Packard 400

44D Pontiac Chieftain

44E Pontiac Star Chief

44B Plymouth Belvedere

44C Plymouth Belvedere

44A : **Packard**, now merged with Studebaker, again offered regular and Clipper models, the latter being the lower-priced line. Illustrated is the luxurious Packard 400 Hardtop. In addition to new body styling and a new 260-bhp V8 engine it featured Torsion-Level ride, a revolutionary new suspension system incorporating long torsion bars interconnecting the front and rear wheels with automatic load-sensitive height/level control.

44B : **Plymouth** P-26-2 Belvedere Six. 1955 models were entirely new and available with a V8 for the first time. The new Hy-Fire engine came in two versions : 157-bhp 241 CID and 167-bhp 260 CID. With optional four-barrel carburettor the 260 CID gave 177 bhp. There were Plaza, Savoy and Belvedere models, all with 115-in wb. Series designations were P-26 for the Sixes, P-27 for the V8s.

44C : **Plymouth** P-27-2 Belvedere Hardtop Coupé. Most Plymouth models were available also as DeSoto (Diplomat) and Dodge (Kingsway), but only for export.

44D : **Pontiac** Series 27 Chieftain 870 Sedan had entirely new body styling with panoramic windscreen and a new overhead-valve V8 engine of 180 bhp rating. There were eight models in this Series and wb was 122 in.

44E : **Pontiac** Series 28 Star Chief Convertible was one of four models in Pontiac's luxury range. Wheelbase was 124 in and the car was powered by the new 287·2 CID 180-bhp Strato-Streak V8.

45A Studebaker Commander

45B Studebaker Commander

45C Studebaker President

45A : **Studebaker** Commander V8 Regal Ultra Vista four-door Sedan, Model 16G8-W6, had 162-bhp 259·2 CID Bearcat V8 engine (High-Power kit optional, 182 bhp). Wheelbase 116·5 in.

45B : **Studebaker** Commander V8 Regal Conestoga Ultra Vista Station Wagon, Model 16G8-D6. It was also available in the less luxurious Champion 16G6 Series (with 185 CID 101-bhp flat-head Six engine).

45C : **Studebaker** revived the old President name for its top-line models. Presidents had a 185-bhp Passmaster V8 engine which was, actually, the Commander's Bearcat with four- (instead of two-) barrel carburettor, and 120-in wb. Illustrated is the special Speedster version of the Hardtop Coupé, one of the immediate predecessors of Stude's famed Hawk sports-type cars.

45D : **Willys** 4 × 4 Jeep Station Wagon and derivations. The last Aero-Willys cars were the Bermuda and Custom with the Hurricane 6 F-head engine. They had a new grille and various minor trim changes. (The name Aero-Willys reappeared, however, in Brazil where Willys-Overland do Brasil SA had commenced Jeep production in 1954 and later introduced the Aero-Willys 2600 Sedan, the Willys-Interlagos Sports Car, and others).

45D Willys Jeep

1956

Most 1956 models differed only slightly from those of the 1955 model year but a new fashion began to emerge—tail fins. Still fairly rudimentary, they continued to 'grow' until by the end of the decade on some cars they had become so large as to be undesirably cumbersome, if not dangerous.

1956 Chrysler Corporation cars featured larger engines, push button automatic transmission controls and 12-volt electrics. Ford also introduced 12 volts as well as a bigger engine (Fairlane with Thunderbird V8), optional safety belts and a new high-quality car, the Continental. General Motors now offered four-door hardtops in all its car division's lines. This body style was becoming increasingly popular and accounted for a large slice of the year's total passenger car sales, which was, nevertheless over a million down on 1955 but still amounted to a staggering 5,816,109.

It is interesting to note that in 1956 Ford Motor Company stock became available to the public for the first time when the Ford Foundation offered more than 10 million of its shares at $64.50 each. The first public stockholders' meeting took place in May.

46B Buick Special

46A Buick Special

46A : **Buick** offered four series : 40 Special, 50 Super, 60 Century and 70 Roadmaster. All models had a 352 CID V8 engine, new front suspension, rear axle and other chassis improvements. Shown : Series 40 Special Sedan, Model 41.

46B : **Buick** Estate Wagon was available in both the 220-bhp Special (shown) and 255-bhp Century Series. Dynaflow was standard on Centurys, optional on Specials.

46C : **Buick** Series 50 Super four-door Hardtop. This model was available in the 50 and 70 Series for the first time this year. They had the 255-bhp engine with variable-pitch Dynaflow and PAS as standard equipment.

46C Buick Super

47A Cadillac

47B Cadillac Eldorado

47C Chevrolet Bel Air

47A: **Cadillac** Coupé de Ville. 1956 styling changes were relatively minor but engine and transmission were further improved. The new 365 CID engine developed 285 bhp and the Hydra-Matic had a 'dump-and-fill' controlled coupling. Power brakes, with 18-in wide pedal, were standard equipment on all models.

47B: **Cadillac** Eldorado Biarritz Convertible (and Seville Hardtop Coupé) had 305-bhp 365 CID V8 engine with 9·75:1 CR, and dual four-barrel carburettors. These high-performance models had distinguishing rear wings, flowing rearward to newly styled oval exhaust ports.

47C: **Chevrolet** Series 2400 Bel Air Convertible, model 2434. 1956 range comprised some 20 models in Special (1500), DeLuxe (2100) and Bel Air (2400) series. Engine options included V8s and a more powerful Six.

47D: **Chevrolet** Series 2900 Corvette, Model 2934, as produced during 1956–57 featured revised styling with concave side panels in the plastic body, power-operated top and side windows and other improvements. It was powered by the 225-bhp Turbofire Special V8. For winter driving there was an optional plastic hardtop (shown).

47D Chevrolet Corvette

1956

48A : **Chrysler** C-71 Windsor Convertible. All Windsors, incl. Nassau and Newport hardtop models had a 331 CID Spitfire V8 engine, rated at 225 bhp, and, like the C-72 Series, 126-in wb.

48B : **Chrysler** C-72 New Yorker Sedan. New Yorkers, including Newport and St. Regis hardtop models, featured 280-bhp 354 CID Firepower V8, push-button PowerFlite transmission, Power Smooth brakes and other refinements. Optional equipment included air-conditioning, instant gasoline heater which reached 100 degrees in seconds, and record player.

48C : **Chrysler** 300B high-performance Hardtop Coupé C-72-300

had increased horsepower, now up to 340 (355 optional). In 1955 a Chrysler 300 won both NASCAR and AAA Stock Car Championships. Like all other 1956 Chryslers it had 12-volt electrics and 126-in wb. Height was 58·6 inches.

48D : **Continental** Mark II was Ford's ultra-luxury prestige car. There was only one model, a two-door hardtop Coupé, Model YA-60. A convertible version by Derham was offered later. The 300-bhp V8 engine, Turbo Drive automatic transmission and other mechanical components were the same as on the Lincoln Capri and Premiere.

48A Chrysler Windsor

48C Chrysler 300B

48B Chrysler New Yorker

48D Continental Mark II

49A : **DeSoto** Diplomat SP-28-1, Diplomat DeLuxe SP-28-2 and Diplomat Custom SP-28-3 (shown) had 125-bhp PowerFlow Six engine. Diplomat SP-29 V8 models had V-motif on grille and 187-bhp Hy-Fire engine. A less powerful V8 export model, designated SP-29X, was available also.

49B : **DeSoto** S-24 Fireflite four-door Sedan. Like the S-23 Firedome it had 126-in wb and a 330 CID V8 engine. The top-line Adventurer, a limited-production hardtop coupé, had a 320-bhp 341·4 CID engine. Fireflites had push-button operated auto.trans. as standard (optional on Firedomes).

49C : **Dodge** introduced a new four-door Hardtop, the Lancer. Shown is the Custom Royal D-63-3 version, but the same body style was offered in the lower-priced Royal D-63-2 and Coronet D-63-1 Series. V8 engines of various bhp ratings were available, but the Coronet could also be bought as a Six (D-62-1). All had 120-in wb. Dodge Kingsway D-49 export models had similar front end styling but smaller engines and 115-in wb.

49D : **Dodge** Custom Sierra four-door Station Wagon was available with two or three seats ; the latter seated eight. Two-door station wagons were named Suburban.

49A DeSoto Diplomat

49B DeSoto Fireflite

49C Dodge Custom Royal

49D Dodge Custom Sierra

1956

50A: **Ford** 1956 models were facelifted editions of the previous year's range but there were some changes in model availability. The Customline Country Sedan 8-pass. Wagon was discontinued, and three new models were added in the Fairlane range: Victoria Fordor (57A, Ford's first four-door hardtop), Parklane Ranch Wagon (59C) and Victoria (64C, shown). The 292 CID V8 engine which powered last year's Thunderbird was now available for other models as well. It developed 202 bhp. The smaller 272 CID V8 and the 223 CID Six now produced 173 and 137 bhp resp.

50B: **Ford** Thunderbird featured an outside spare wheel. There was choice of two engines: Thunderbird Y-8 292 CID for gearshift models (202 bhp) and Thunderbird Special Y-8 312 CID for cars with overdrive (215 bhp) and Fordomatic (225 bhp).

50C: **Hudson** cars were again based on contemporary Nashes. The Wasp (shown) was powered by the 202 CID Six engine that had been used in the Hudson Jet prior to the merger with Nash, when the Jet was superseded by the Nash Rambler with Hudson name plates. For the Hornet AMC used the Packard V8 power unit, as in 1955.

50D: **Imperial** four-door Sedan of the 133-in wb C-73 Series. Other body styles were new Southampton two- and four-door Hardtops. The FirePower 9·0:1 CR 354 CID V8 developed 280 bhp and auto.trans. (PowerFlite), PAB and PAS were standard equipment. The C-70 Crown Imperial had 149½-in wb.

50B Ford Thunderbird

50C Hudson Wasp

50A Ford Fairlane

50D Imperial

51A Lincoln Premiere

51D Metropolitan

51B Mercury Montclair

51C Meteor Rideau

51A: **Lincoln** Premiere Convertible, Model LD-76B. Other models: 60B Coupé and 73B Sedan. Capri range comprised 60E Sport Coupé and 73A Sedan. All had 126-in wb, PAS and new 285-bhp 368 CID V8 with 9·0:1 CR. Push-button lubrication system for front suspension and steering was optional.

51B: **Mercury** Montclair Hardtop Sedan, also known as Phaeton, was one of Mercury's four top-line models. Other series comprised Monterey with four models and Custom with five. 5·1-litre V8 delivered 210, 215 or 225 bhp, depending on model and transmission type.

51C: **Meteor** Rideau Sedan. The Meteor, produced by Ford Canada from 1948, was claimed to be the only North American car sold exclusively in Canada.

51D: **Metropolitan** Series 1500 Convertible 561 and Hardtop 562, made for AMC by Austin of England, were modified in various respects. Radio, heater and lighter were standard. Three-speed transmission had dash-mounted control. Engine was Austin A50 1500-cc. From December they were sold outside North America as Austin Metropolitan 1500.

51E: **Nash** offered one Statesman and seven Ambassador models, the latter with Special, Six and V8 variants. Specials had a new AMC 190-bhp V8 and were announced in April. Rambler became a separate marque (See 53C).

51E Nash Ambassador

1956

52A : **Oldsmobile** introduced new Jetaway Hydra-Matic Drive and Starfire styling. The Rocket engine's power was increased to 240 bhp. An automatic six-way power seat was made available and in November the three-millionth Hydra-Matic-equipped Olds was produced. Shown is the Series 98 DeLuxe Holiday Coupé.

52B : **Packard**-built Clipper was now on its own and no longer advertised as a small Packard. However, this was the last year of Packard and Clipper as individual cars (see 1957). The Clipper, shown in Super Hardtop Coupé form, had a 240-bhp V8 engine, and torsion bar suspension. A Twin-Traction limited-slip differential was available, for the first time in the medium-price field, on all models.

52C : **Plymouth** Belvedere V8 Sedan. Plaza, Savoy and Belvedere models were offered with six-cylinder (P-28) or V8 (P-29) engines, supplemented by a high-performance Fury two-door Hardtop model in P-29 range. The Six was a 125-bhp 230 CID L-head, the Standard V8 was a 277 CID unit of 187- or 200-bhp rating. Optional was a smaller 270 CID V8 of 180 bhp and the Fury had a 303 CID V8 with 9·25 :1 CR and output of 240 or 270 bhp.

52D : **Plymouth** Belvedere V8 Hardtop Sedan, one of 15 models in Plymouth's 1956 line of cars. Auto.trans., if fitted, had push-button control.

52A Oldsmobile Ninety-Eight

52C Plymouth Belvedere

52B Packard Clipper

52D Plymouth Belvedere

53A : **Pontiac** offered four Series : 860, 870 and Safari with 122-in wb and Star Chief with 124-in wb. All had Strato Streak 316·6 CID V8 engine, developing up to 227 bhp, depending on model and transmission type. Illustrated is 860 Catalina Hardtop Coupé.

53B : **Pontiac** Six. General Motors of Canada produced Pontiac Laurentian (shown) and Pathfinder models, employing Chevrolet mechanical components, including Powerglide.

53C : **Rambler** was now offered as an individual make and offered larger models than hitherto, all on 108-in wb and with 120-bhp OHV

Typhoon Six engine. Shown is the Cross Country Station Wagon. The 'dip' in the roofline was introduced by Nash on their 1954 Rambler four-door wagon. Note : until 1957 American Motors continued *registering* Ramblers as Nash and Hudson cars.

53D : **Willys** continued their range of Jeep vehicles and in October 1955 introduced this low-priced 4 × 2 Model DJ3A Dispatcher, with canvas top (shown), with hardtop (incorporating fibreglass plastic roof and sliding side doors) and as a basic open model. All had the 60-bhp L-head Four Go-Devil engine.

53A Pontiac 860

53C Rambler

53B Pontiac Laurentian

53D Willys Jeep

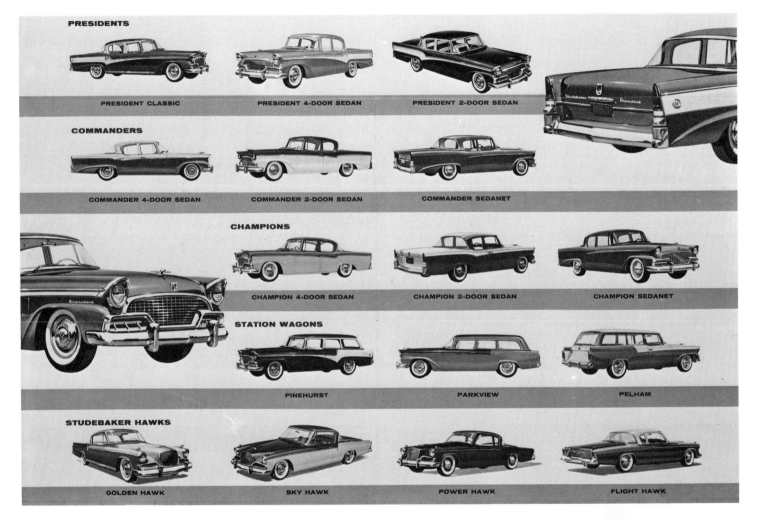

PRESIDENTS

PRESIDENT CLASSIC   PRESIDENT 4-DOOR SEDAN   PRESIDENT 2-DOOR SEDAN

COMMANDERS

COMMANDER 4-DOOR SEDAN   COMMANDER 2-DOOR SEDAN   COMMANDER SEDANET

CHAMPIONS

CHAMPION 4-DOOR SEDAN   CHAMPION 2-DOOR SEDAN   CHAMPION SEDANET

STATION WAGONS

PINEHURST   PARKVIEW   PELHAM

STUDEBAKER HAWKS

GOLDEN HAWK   SKY HAWK   POWER HAWK   FLIGHT HAWK

54 : **Studebaker** offered four lines : Series 56G Champion, 56B Commander, 56H President and 56J Golden Hawk. There were Hawk Coupés in the Champion, Commander and President Series as well, namely 56G Flight Hawk and Silver Hawk, 56B Power Hawk and 56H Skyhawk. Station Wagons were the 56G Pelham, 56B Parkview and 56H Pinehurst. Engines : Sweepstakes 185 CID L-head Six for Champion (incl. Flight Hawk and Pelham), Sweepstakes 259·2 CID V8 for Commander (incl. Power Hawk and Parkview), Sweepstakes 289 CID V8 for President (incl. Skyhawk and Pinehurst) and Skypower 352 CID V8 for Golden Hawk. Outputs ranged from 101 to 275 bhp.

1957

During 1957 the US automotive industry sold 6,113,344 passenger cars and more than one million trucks and buses. Nash and Hudson were in their last year: American Motors discontinued these marque names and concentrated on Ramblers. Plymouth delivered their 10-millionth car, Ford their three-millionth Mercury.

Chrysler Corporation's 1957 cars (Chrysler, DeSoto, Dodge, Imperial, Plymouth) featured torsion bar front suspension and Plymouth nine-passenger station wagons had rear-facing third seat. Most cars now had 14-inch wheels instead of 15-inch which had been customary since the 1940s. Fuel injection engines were available from Chevrolet and Pontiac and several makes offered dual headlights. Ford introduced their Skyliner with retractable metal convertible top. A speedometer buzzer which sounded when a pre-set speed was reached was another new feature for 1957. On the subject of speed, the AMA adopted a resolution to exclude speed and racing from members' automotive publicity.

55B Cadillac 60 Special

55A Buick Century

55C Cadillac Eldorado Brougham

55A : **Buick** Series 60 Century Riviera Hardtop Coupé, Model 66R, was one of four models in this range. It had a 300-bhp V8 engine with 10 :1 CR (8·5 optional). Larger panoramic windscreen, three-piece rear windows, restyled front and rear end and new chassis were among 1957 features. Series 50 Super and 70 Roadmaster had same engine. Series 40 Special had same CID but lower output. Dynaflow was optional on Specials, standard on others.
55B : **Cadillac** Series 60 Special Fleetwood Sedan, Model 6039.

Hardtop four-door bodywork on tubular-centre X-frame. Power-assisted steering and brakes, power operated windows and front seat. 6-litre 279-bhp V8 engine with Hydra-Matic transmission.
55C : **Cadillac** introduced the limited-production luxurious Eldorado Brougham model, with air suspension as standard equipment. The Brougham, which had four headlights, was $55\frac{1}{2}$ inches high, $216\frac{1}{4}$ inches long. The 325-bhp engine had dual four-barrel carburettors and 10 :1 CR. Roof, mouldings and fender skirts were of stainless steel.

1957

56A: **Chevrolet** 1957 models had new front and rear end styling and many other modifications. The wheel size was reduced from 15 to 14 in. Shown is the Series 2400 Bel Air Sport Coupé (hardtop), Model 2454. There was also a four-door Hardtop. Several 'power trains' were available. Corvettes, which retained their 15-in wheels, were similar externally to the 1956 models (q.v.) but available with five V8 engines, ranging from 220 to 283 bhp, including two with fuel injection.
56B: **Chevrolet** Bel Air Nomad Station Wagon. Rear part of bodywork was patterned on that of an experimental wagon based on the Corvette.
56C: **Chrysler** offered four series, all with V8 engines and 126-in wheelbase: Windsor C-75-1 (285-bhp 354 CID), Saratoga C-75-2 (295-bhp 354 CID), New Yorker C-76 (325-bhp 392 CID) and 300C C-76-300 (375-bhp 392 CID). Illustrated is the Saratoga four-door Hardtop which was made with either single or dual headlights.
56D: **Chrysler** 300C scored big repeat performance as Daytona champion. It was optionally available with 390-bhp FirePower V8 (std version: 375 bhp).
56E: **Continental**, élite car of Ford's Lincoln-Mercury Division, was not much different from 1956 offering. After 1957 Continental became the top model of the Lincoln line, rather than a separate marque.

56C Chrysler Saratoga

56D Chrysler 300C

56A Chevrolet Bel Air

56B Chevrolet Bel Air Nomad

56E Continental Mark II

57A DeSoto Diplomat

57B DeSoto Fireflite

57A : **DeSoto** Diplomat was available with Six (SP-30, SP-30X) and V8 (SP-31, SP-31X) engines ranging from 132 to 235 bhp. Overdrive and PowerFlite auto. trans. were optional (TorqueFlite only on Diplomat Custom V8). Basically they were 118-in wb Plymouths. Diplomat Station Wagons had 122-in wb.

57B : **DeSoto** S-26 Fireflite Sportsman Hardtop Coupé had 295-bhp 341 CID V8 engine. Like the Firedome (S-25, 270-bhp) and Adventurer (S-26, 345-bhp) it had 126-in wb.

57C : **DeSoto** Fireflite Sedan. A new lower-priced series this year was the FireSweep with 245- or 260-bhp V8 and 122-in wb. It accounted for 35% of the total DeSoto production by the end of the model year.

57D : **Dodge** Royal Hardtop. 1957 models featured Torsion-Aire front suspension with torsion bars. 14-inch wheels allowed bigger tyres than the previous 15-inch. Available were Coronet D-66, Royal D-67-1 and Custom Royal D-67-2 models as well as Suburban and Sierra D-70 and Custom Sierra D-71 station wagons, all with V8 Red Ram engines. Sixes comprised Coronet and Coronet Custom D-72-1 and -2 models. All had 122-in wb.

57E : **Dodge** Kingsway Six and V8 ranges were technically similar to corresponding Plymouth and DeSoto Diplomat models, with 122-in wb for station wagons, 118-in for other variants. Shown : Kingsway Custom Sedan.

57D Dodge Royal

57E Dodge Kingsway

57C DeSoto Fireflite

1957

58A Ford Custom 300

58B Ford Fairlane 500

58C Ford Fairlane 500

58A : **Ford** Custom 300 Fordor, Model 73B. There were three passenger car series : Fairlane (incl. Fairlane 500), Custom (incl. Custom 300) and Station Wagons. In addition there were the Custom Ranchero Pickup and Courier Sedan Delivery, and the 'T-birds'. Four engines were available : 223 CID Mileage Maker Six (144-bhp), and 272, 292 and 312 V8s (up to 245-bhp). Fairlanes had 118-in wb, others 116-in. Custom and Custom 300 replaced earlier Mainline and Customline resp. All models had 14-in wheels with 7·50 or 8·00-14 tyres.

58B : **Ford** Fairlane 500 Sunliner Convertible, Model 76B.

58C : **Ford** Fairlane 500 Skyliner Retractable Hardtop, Model 51A, was new and cost almost $3000. The top could be retracted automatically into the luggage compartment. For this purpose the boot (deck) lid was rear-hinged.

58D : **Ford** Fairlane 500 Country Sedan 79C was very popular and, it was claimed, helped Ford to sell more station wagons than all other auto makers together. There were five models, as well as two-door Ranch Wagons.

58E : **Ford** Thunderbird had a new front bumper and other, less eyecatching, changes. Engine options were 292 and 312 CID V8s of 212 and 245 bhp, wb 102 in.

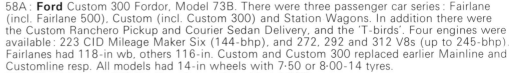

58D Ford Fairlane 500

58E Ford Thunderbird

59A : **Hudson** Hornet four-door Sedan was powered by American Motors' new V8 engine (255 bhp, 327 CID, CR 9·0:1) It was one of the last Hudsons. After the 1957 model year AMC concentrated on the production of the smaller Rambler models.

59B : **Imperial** Crown Southampton Hardtop. 1957 models had new bodywork with compound curved windscreen and curved side windows. Either single or dual headlights could be fitted. There were three series : IM1-1 Imperial, IM1-2 Imperial Crown and IM1-4 Imperial LeBaron, all with 129-in wb, 325-bhp 329 CID V8 engine, TorqueFlite transmission, PAB and PAS.

59C : **Lincoln** LD-57B Premiere Landau Pillarless Sedan. Other Premieres were 58B Sedan, 60B Hardtop and 76B Convertible Coupés. Capri range comprised 58A Sedan, 57A Pillarless Sedan and 60A Hardtop Coupé. Lincoln also produced the ultra-luxurious Continental (q.v.). All had 300-bhp V8 and Turbo Drive.

59D : **Mercury** offered three entirely new series : Monterey (shown), Montclair and Station Wagons. 255-bhp 5·1-litre Safety Surge and 290-bhp 6-litre Turnpike Cruiser V8 (Lincoln) engines were available. Bodywork was exclusive to Mercury for the first time, rather than based on other Ford bodyshells.

59E : **Meteor** continued as a Canadian-built adaptation of the US Ford. Model shown resembled Ford Fairlane Hardtop.

59C Lincoln Premiere

59D Mercury Monterey

59A Hudson Hornet

59B Imperial Crown

59E Meteor Rideau

60A : **Nash** Ambassador V8 Series was the only Nash line for 1957, and the last. Henceforth only Rambler cars were made. Illustrated is the Ambassador Custom four-door Sedan. Also available was a two-door Hardtop, as well as Super variants of both.

60B : **Oldsmobile** Golden Rocket Series 88 Holiday Coupé. Many styling changes were introduced, including sculptured rear fenders and twin-strut (three-piece) rear windows. The 371 CID Rocket V8 developed 277 bhp. In January the J-2 Rocket engine with three dual carburettors was introduced. It could develop 300 bhp or more. An engineering 'first' was the printed electric circuit for the instrument cluster.

60C : **Oldsmobile** Starfire Series 98 Holiday Sedan was among Olds' top-line models. Wheelbase of 98 and 88 models was 126 and 122 in resp.

60D : **Oldsmobile** Super 88 Holiday Coupé; close-up showing three-piece rear window lay-out which was also a feature of Olds' British GM cousins, the Vauxhall PA Series Velox and Cresta.

60E : **Oldsmobile** Super 88 Fiesta Station Wagon.

60C Oldsmobile Ninety-Eight

60D Oldsmobile Super 88

60A Nash Ambassador

60B Oldsmobile 88

60E Oldsmobile Super 88

61A : **Packard** had now become a 'Packardized' Studebaker and only two models were offered : 57L-Y Clipper Town Sedan (shown) and 57L-P Clipper Country Sedan (station wagon). Engine was 275-bhp 289 CID V8. Most had Studebaker's Flightomatic transmission but three-speed manual with Warner overdrive was available if desired.

61B : **Plymouth** P-31-3 Belvedere Sedan had 301 CID V8 of 215 or 235 bhp, or, as P-30-3, a 230 CID L-head Six of 132-bhp rating. Plazas, Savoys and Belvederes had 118-in, Suburbans (wagons) 122-in wb. TorqueFlite auto.trans. was available at extra cost. Over 600,000 Plymouths were produced this year, including the 10-millionth.

61C : **Plymouth** P-31-3 Belvedere Hardtop Coupé with V8 Hy-Fire engine. The Fury model had a 318 CID V8, developing 290 bhp. All Plymouths had torsion bar IFS.

61D : **Plymouth** sedans were popular for police and taxicab use in many cities. This Savoy, operated by Fleetway Cabs of Baltimore, Md, was powered by a British Perkins P4(C) 4-cyl. diesel engine.

61E : **Pontiac** Series 28 Star Chief Custom Catalina Hardtop Sedan, one of five body styles available in this 124-in wb top-line range. Star Flight exterior styling was available in 68 colour combinations. All Series 27 models (Chieftain, Super Chief and Star Chief) had 122-in wb. Wheel size was down from 15 to 14 in.

61B Plymouth Belvedere

61C Plymouth Belvedere

61A Packard Clipper

61D Plymouth Savoy

61E Pontiac Star Chief

1957

62A: **Rambler** 1957 range comprised Six and V8 models, all on 108-in wheelbase. Shown is a Custom V8 four-door Sedan, Model 5725-2. Of the 118,990 cars built by AM in 1957, 114,084 were Ramblers, the rest were (the last) Hudsons and Nashes. Included in the Ramblers were 1500 high-performance Rebel four-door Custom Hardtops. These had AM's new 255-bhp 327 CID V8 and silver paint finish with gold-anodized 'spears' (side flashes).

62B: **Studebaker** offered 57G Champion, 57B Commander and 57H President and Golden Hawk Series. The President Classic Sedan (shown), which was also available as a Packard (*q.v.*), was Studebaker's lead model and had a 225-bhp V8 and Twin-Traction limited-slip differential. For the first time there were four-door Station Wagons, namely the Provincial (57B and H) and Broadmoor (57H). Pelham

(57G) and Parkview (57B and H) two-door wagons were continued.

62C: **Studebaker** Golden Hawk Model 57H-K7 was top-line sports-type five-seater Hardtop, only 56 in high but 17 feet long. It had a 275-bhp 289 CID V8 power plant with centrifugal type McCulloch supercharger. Also available were Silver Hawks, with Six and V8 engines (57B, G and H). All had 120½-in wheelbase.

62D: **Willys** supplied Universal and other Jeep vehicles to civilian customers and governments all over the world. Many were produced or assembled overseas. Typical of the Universal range was this Model CJ6, long-wheelbase (101 in) variant of the CJ5. In military guise it saw service as a field ambulance (MDA; Truck, ¼-ton, 4 × 4, Ambulance, Front Line, M170). The CJ6 was first announced in November 1955.

62A Rambler Custom

62B Studebaker President

62C Studebaker Golden Hawk

62D Willys Jeep

63A Buick Century

63B Buick Century

63C Cadillac 60 Special

1958

Passenger car sales during 1958 were down again, to just over 4¼-million. Truck sales were down also, to under 900,000.

General Motors and Ford celebrated golden anniversaries. Ford commemorated theirs, i.e. their Model T's, by reassembling a 1909 'Tin Lizzy', and produced their 50-millionth vehicle. Ford also introduced the Edsel car, which featured push button automatic transmission controls in the centre of the steering wheel, self-adjusting brakes and other attractions. The car did not live up to Ford's expectations, however, and was discontinued in November, 1959.

Chrysler Corp. produced its 25-millionth vehicle. Most 1958 cars had dual headlights with four 5¾-in 'Sealed Beam' units. Air suspension was optional equipment on all General Motors' car makes and both Chrysler and Cadillac offered a device designed to hold a car at a preselected speed. Optional on Chrysler's Imperial were 11.00–14 tyres, claimed to be the largest passenger car tyres in the world.

Studebaker-Packard decided to drastically curtail their production programme and to concentrate on their new Lark compact car.

63D Cadillac 62 Eldorado

63A: **Buick** Series 60 Century Convertible, Model 66C was one of 20 models in five series: 40 Special, 50 Super, 60 Century, 75 Roadmaster and the new 700 Limited. All models had a new and unusual radiator grille and dual headlights. The 'port-holes' had disappeared.

63B: **Buick** Series 60 Century Caballero Station Wagon, Model 69, featured hardtop bodystyling.

63C: **Cadillac** Series 60 Special Fleetwood Sedan, Model 6039. Among the features which distinguished it from other Cadillacs were the extruded aluminium shields at the bottom of the rear quarter panels and the stainless steel moulding extending over the bottom of the doors. Wheelbase of this model was 133 inches, overall length 225·3. All models were optionally available with air suspension.

63D: **Cadillac** Series 62 Eldorado Biarritz Convertible, Model 6267S, and its hardtop companion, the Seville, had a silhouette and rear view distinctively different from other models.

1958

64A : **Checker** taxicab, from Kalamazoo, Mich., was of straightforward and sturdy design, with L-head Six engine.

64B : **Chevrolet** range was entirely revised and came in three series, with Six/V8 engines : Delray (1100/1200), Biscayne (1500/1600) and luxury Bel Air (1700/1800). In addition to Powerglide, Turboglide transmission was optional on V8s. Other options included PAS, PAB, Positraction self-locking differential and Level Air suspension. Shown, are the Sport Sedan, Model 1839, Impala Sport Coupé, 1847 and

Impala Convertible, 1867, all from the Bel Air 1800 Series.

64C : **Chevrolet** Nomad four-door Station Wagon, Model 1893 (1793 with 6-cyl. engine). Other 1958 wagons were the two- and four-door Yeoman and four-door Brookwood.

64D : **Chevrolet** Corvette Sports Roadster, Model 867, had new front with dual headlights and other styling changes. 3- or 4-speed manual or Powerglide trans. could be specified, with four versions of the Super Turbo Fire V8 engine.

64A Checker Cab

64B Chevrolet Bel Air

64C Chevrolet Nomad

64D Chevrolet Corvette

65A Chrysler Windsor

65B Chrysler Saratoga

65A : Chrysler Windsor four-door Hardtop Sedan, LC1-L-43, was one of five models in the 122-in wheelbase LC1-L Series. Their 354 CID Spitfire V8 engine had 10:1 CR and developed 290 bhp.

65B : Chrysler Saratoga two-door Hardtop Coupé, LC2-M-23. There were two other models in the LC2-M Series : conventional and hardtop four-door sedans. They had a 310-bhp 354 CID Spitfire V8 engine and 126-in wheelbase.

65C : Chrysler top-line series was New Yorker LC3-H, with 345-bhp 392 CID V8, 126-in wheelbase and six body styles (Sedan shown). High-performance 300D (LC3-S) had 380-bhp engine or optional 390-bhp unit with fuel injection.

65D : DeSoto Diplomat Six LF1 and V8 LF2 Series resembled Plymouth except for distinguishing grille and badges. Standard, DeLuxe and Custom models were available, albeit only in certain export markets. They had 118-in wb except station wagons (122-in). Shown : Diplomat DeLuxe Hardtop Sedan, Model LF1-M-43.

65E : DeSoto Fireflite Sportsman Hardtop Sedan, Model LS3-H-43, shared 126-in wb chassis and 361 CID V8 engine with Series LS2-M Firedome and LS3-S Adventurer but horsepower ratings differed. FireSweep (LS1-L) had 122-in wb and 350 CID V8 engines. All had 10:1 CR except Adventurer (10·25:1) which was available with fuel injection also.

65F : Dodge Custom Royal LD3-H Convertible. 1958 Dodges had restyled grille, dual headlights, compound-curved windscreens and other styling changes. Electronic fuel injection system was available, boosting power output to 333 bhp. Of US produced Dodges in 1958, 96·4% had automatic transmission, 62·5% had PAS, 34% had PAB. The Coronet range (LD1 Six and LD2 V8) accounted for 70% of all sales.

65C Chrysler New Yorker

65E DeSoto Fireflite

65D DeSoto Diplomat

65F Dodge Custom Royal

1958

66A Dodge Sierra

66A: **Dodge** LD-3 Sierra was one of five station wagons offered. Two-door models were known as Suburban. Sierra Spectator variants had rear-facing third seat.

66B: **Edsel** Citation Hardtop and Convertible were two models in a new line introduced by Ford in the medium price field ('priced from just above the lowest to just below the highest'). It was claimed that the Edsel was the result of eleven years of planning and testing, including more than 1,250,000 test miles. However, although styling and controls had some unusual features, the technical specification was much like that of other contemporary Ford-produced cars. There are 18 models, incl. five station wagons, in four Series: Ranger, Pacer, Corsair and Citation.

66C Edsel Citation

66D Ford Fairlane 500

66C: **Edsel** Citation four-door Hardtop was top-line model. Equipment included self-adjusting brakes, push button auto.trans. controls in centre of steering wheel and floating drum-type speedometer. Options included dash-mounted compass, tachometer, etc. Engines were E-400 361 CID 303-bhp V8 for Ranger, Pacer and Station Wagons, E-475 410 CID 345-bhp V8 for Corsair and Citation.

66D: **Ford** 1958 front and rear end styling was changed dramatically and featured dual head and tail lights. Body side mouldings were also redesigned. Illustrated is the Fairlane 500 Sunliner Convertible, Model 76B. Engines were 145-bhp Mileage Maker Six and 240-, 265- and 300-bhp Interceptor V8s. Transmission: conventional, overdrive and Fordomatic or Cruise-O-Matic automatic.

66E: **Ford** Fairlane 500 Sunliner rear view, showing dual tail lights and exhausts. Ford-Aire suspension was optional on V8s with automatic transmission.

66F: **Ford** Thunderbird was entirely restyled for the first time. It was now a four-seater prestige model, rather than a sports car, and the body was of unitary construction. Convertible and Hardtop (shown) body styles were available. 300-bhp Thunderbird 352 Special V8 was standard but for export a 235-bhp engine was offered.

66B Edsel Citation

66E Ford Fairlane 500

66F Ford Thunderbird

67A Imperial Crown

67B Kaiser Carabela

67C Lincoln Capri

67A: Imperial Crown LY1-M Southampton four-door Hardtop with Landau top roof section and FliteSweep rear deck (boot) lid with simulated spare wheel cover. There were also Imperial LY1-L and Imperial LeBaron LY1-H models. All had 129-in wb and 345-bhp 392 CID engine with 10:1 CR.

67B: Kaiser Carabela, Model KA1, was South American continuation of the 1954/55 North American Manhattan Sedan. It was produced, until the 1960s, by Industrias Kaiser Argentina SA in Buenos Aires, to where all the body dies and other tooling had been transferred. IKA also produced various Willys Jeep models (*q.v.*).

67C: Lincoln Capri Landau. 1958 models were completely restyled and featured unitary body-cum-chassis construction. The 7-litre V8 had 10·5:1 CR and developed 375 bhp. Body styles in the Capri and Premiere lines were the same, namely four-door Sedans (53A), Landau Hardtop Sedans (63A) and Hardtop Coupés (57A and B resp.).

67D: Lincoln Continental was no longer sold as a separate marque, as in 1956–57. It was Lincoln's top-line model and designated Mark III it was available as Coupé, Landau (hardtop sedan), Sedan, and Convertible (shown).

67E: Mercury Park Lane Phaeton Sedan was one of 20 models offered for 1958. It was 220¼ in long and the wheelbase was 125 in. Coupé and Convertible models were also available. Other series were the Montclair, Monterey and Station Wagons, with various body, engine and transmission options. Air Cushion Ride air suspension was among the optional extras.

67D Lincoln Continental

67E Mercury Park Lane

68A Meteor Rideau

68B Oldsmobile Dynamic 88

68C Oldsmobile Ninety-Eight

68D Packard

68E Packard Hawk

68A: **Meteor** Rideau 500 four-door Hardtop was one of the cars produced by Ford of Canada, using US Ford Fairlane components but carrying their own distinguishing grille, badges and trim.
68B: **Oldsmobile** offered Dynamic 88, Super 88 and 98 models. Illustrated is the four-door Holiday Sedan of the Dynamic 88 Series. Completely restyled, 1958 Oldsmobiles had dual headlamps, aluminium grille, new decorative trim on the side panels and choice of three 371 CID Rocket engines, ranging from 265 to 312 bhp depending on carburettor specification. Optional equipment included New-Matic Ride air suspension and Trans-Portable (easily-removable) radio.
68C: **Oldsmobile** 98 Convertible Coupé. Series 98 had 126½-in wb, Dynamic 88 and Super 88 122½-in.
68D: **Packard** entered its last year of existence with three regular models: 58L-Y8 Town Sedan (shown), 58L-J8 Hardtop Coupé and 58L-P8 Station Wagon. They were based on the Studebaker President and powered by a 225-bhp 289 CID V8 (Studebaker Sweepstakes 289). Transmission was Flightomatic or manual with overdrive. Not surprisingly, sales were dismal.
68E: **Packard** Hawk Coupé, Model 58L-K9, was attractive but not different enough from the Studebaker Golden Hawk, which it resembled technically, to keep the marque alive. If anything, the Stude looked better. Both had a supercharged 289 CID V8 with a maximum output of 275 bhp at 4800 rpm.

69A: **Plymouth** LP2-H Fury was available only as two-door Hardtop. It had gold-coloured anodized aluminium inserts between the body side mouldings. Engine was the Dual Fury V-800 or optional Golden Commando (up to 315 bhp with fuel injection).

69B: **Plymouth** Sport Suburban V8, Model LP2-H-45. Series designation was LP1 for Sixes, LP2 for V8s. Model ranges were Plaza, Savoy, Belvedere and Fury cars, Suburban, Custom Suburban and Sport Suburban wagons. Engine outputs ranged from 132 to 315 bhp.

69C: **Pontiac** Star Chief Catalina four-door Hardtop. There were Chieftain, Super Chief, Star Chief and Bonneville Series. The latter was new for 1958. Output of the new 370 CID Tempest 395 V8 ranged from 240 up to 310 bhp with fuel injection and Super Hydra-Matic.

69D: **Rambler** American was new 100-in wb small car of AMC. It had a 195·6 CID 90-bhp L-head Six and was $178\frac{1}{4}$ in long.

69E: **Rambler** Rebel Custom Country Club Hardtop Sedan, Model 5829-2, had 108-in wb and 215-bhp V8. Top-line Ambassadors had 117-in and 270-bhp resp.

69F: **Rambler** Rebel V8 Cross Country Station Wagons featured distinctive notched roof line and chrome travel rack.

69C Pontiac Star Chief

69D Rambler American

69A Plymouth Fury

69E Rambler Rebel

69B Plymouth Sport Suburban

69F Rambler Rebel

1958

70A Studebaker Scotsman

70B Studebaker President

70C Studebaker Silver Hawk

70D Willys/IKA Jeep

70E Willys/IKA Jeep

70A: **Studebaker** Scotsman Station Wagon, 58G-D1, was one of a new line, introduced as 'America's lowest-priced full sized automobile'. They were, in effect, austere versions of the Champion. Series designation for Scotsman and Champion lines was 58G. All had the flat-head Six Sweepstakes 185 engine, rated at 101 bhp. First Studebaker Econ-o-miler taxicab also made its debut this year.

70B: **Studebaker** President six-passenger two-door Hardtop, Model 58H-J6. A four-door sedan was also available (58H-Y6).

70C: **Studebaker** Silver Hawk was available in the Champion Series with 6-cyl. engine as Model 58G-C3 (shown) and in the President Series with V8 engine as 58H-C3 Hardtop. Golden Hawk Series 58H-K7 continued as Stude's top-line sports-type car with supercharged Sweepstakes 289 V8 engine, developing 275 bhp at 4800 rpm.

70D: **Willys** was one of the world's largest four-wheel drive vehicle makers and a wide range of models was available. Industrias Kaiser Argentina in Buenos Aires produced various Willys models, including the Estanciera Station Wagon (4 × 4: UA-1RA, 4 × 2: UA-1RB) and various Jeep types (4 × 4: JA-1MA, 4 × 2: JA-3UB, Convertible 4 × 2: JA-3CB). Shown is the JA-1MA, which was similar to the US-made CJ5 Universal.

70E: **Willys** Jeep Model JA-3CB was Argentinian derivative of the North American CJ5 Universal, featuring built-in side steps, chrome bumpers and wheel hub covers as well as removable doors and convertible top. On this model, which was exclusive to the Argentine, only the rear axle was driven, and consequently the usual Jeep transfer case was not fitted.

1959

Total passenger car sales for the year amounted to 5,591,243. Pontiac produced their 7-millionth vehicle and Chrysler reorganized their car sales division by forming the Plymouth-DeSoto Division, the Chrysler-Imperial Division and the Dodge Division. Following the lead of the smaller 'independents', who during the 1950s had introduced small cars with varying degrees of success (Hudson Jet, Kaiser Henry J, Nash Rambler, Studebaker Lark, Willys Aero) and the increasing impact of 'imports' (mainly Volkswagen) on the home market, the 'big three' had decided that the time was ripe to start competing in this field and late in 1959 introduced what became generally known as the 'compacts': General Motors launched their Chevrolet Corvair, Ford their Falcon and Chrysler their Plymouth Valiant. They were introduced as 1960 models. It meant that from now on the two main types of American cars were 'compact' and 'regular' models (during the next decade to be joined by the 'intermediates').

Cadillac offered Cruise-Control automatic acceleration, maintaining a pre-set speed whether going uphill or downhill.

71A Buick LeSabre

71B Cadillac 62

71C Chevrolet Impala

71A: **Buick** 1959 models were entirely new. Four-door hardtop models had a flat roof line with large curved rear window as exemplified by this LeSabre. All had a new compound (curved in both planes) windscreen. There were three series: LeSabre 4400, Invicta 4600 and Electra 4700/4800. Two-door Buicks featured a locking device to prevent the back of the front passenger seat from suddenly moving forward.

71B: **Cadillac** offered option of two body styles in their Series 62 Sedan and Sedan de Ville series: a six-window and a four-window type, with distinctive roof contours. Shown is the Six-Window Sedan. Series 62 and 60 now had same 130-in wheelbase. Total production of Series 62, 60 and 75: 142,272.

71C: **Chevrolet** Series 1800 Impala Sport Sedan, Model 1839, also had GM's new flat roof hardtop style with large wrap-around rear window.

1959

72A: **Chevrolet** Series 1500 Bel Air Sedan, Model 1519 (with V8 engine : Model 1619). Other series were low-price Biscayne 1100 Six and 1200 V8 and luxury Impala 1700 Six and 1800 V8. All models had compound-curve panoramic windscreens, large tail fins and 119-in wb.

72B: **Chevrolet** Corvette Sports Roadster was similar in appearance to 1958 model. Body was made entirely from plastic. Most powerful engine available was 294-bhp V8 with 10·5:1 CR and fuel injection.

72C Chrysler Windsor

72D Chrysler New Yorker

72E: **Chrysler** 300E, Series MC3-H, had 380-bhp version of Golden Lion 413 CID V8. All had 10:1 CR, but for export lower ratios were available on most models.

72F: **Chrysler** cars ceased to be available in Australia in 1952 but in 1957 an Australian-built range, named Royal AP1, was introduced, originally with 25·35 and 28·35-HP (RAC) L-head Sixes. Later a V8 (48·05 HP, 220 bhp, 313 CID) was added and the small Six dropped. Shown is the Royal Big Six, Series AP3, with 28·35-HP (117-bhp) PowerFlow engine. TorqueFlite was standard on the V8, optional on the Six. All had 115-in wb.

72A Chevrolet Bel Air

72B Chevrolet Corvette

72C: **Chrysler** Windsor, Series MC1-L, two-door Hardtop was powered by a new 305-bhp Golden Lion 383 engine. New two-tone roof, push button air conditioner and heater controls, torsion bar front suspension and extra large rear window were among its features. Swivel front seats were optional on many Chrysler Corp. cars.

72D: **Chrysler** New Yorker, Series MC3-H, had new 350-bhp Golden Lion 413 engine. The new power units, all V8s, had wedge-shaped combustion chambers, replacing the 1951–58 'hemi-head' FirePower. Shown is the four-door Hardtop. Like the intermediate Saratoga, Series MC2-M, they had 126-in wb.

72E Chrysler 300E

72F Chrysler Royal (Australia)

73A DeSoto Diplomat

73C : **Dodge** Kingsway (export) had similar front end to regular models but otherwise resembled the Plymouth and DeSoto Diplomat. Shown is the Kingsway Lancer Convertible.
73D : **Dodge** Royal Series MD3-M four-door Sedan had 361 CID V8 engine of 295 bhp ; 320- and 345-bhp power units were optional. Six-cylinder engine was available only in the lowest-price Coronet MD1-L.

73E Dodge Custom Royal

73B DeSoto Fireflite

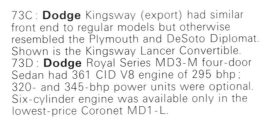

73C Dodge Kingsway

73F Dodge Sierra

73A : **DeSoto** Diplomat Six Series MF1 and V8 MF2 export models had 132-bhp PowerFlow 6 and Fury V-800 engines resp. Certain models were optionally available with 4-cyl. Perkins P4 diesel engines. Manual, overdrive and automatic trans. were offered. Shown is the Diplomat V8 Adventurer Convertible.
73B : **DeSoto** Firedome MS2-M, and Fireflite and Adventurer MS3-H had 126-in wb and larger V8 engine of 383 CID with 10·1 :1 CR. Power output ranged from 305 to 350 bhp. This engine was now also available for the 122-in wb FireSweep, which had 361 CID unit as standard equipment. Illustrated : Model MS3-H-23 Fireflite Sportsman Hardtop Coupé.

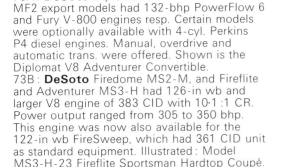

73D Dodge Royal

73E : **Dodge** Custom Royal Series MD3-H four-door Hardtop was top model. Standard engine developed 305 bhp ; 320- and 345-bhp units were optional. Picture shows dramatically the fashionable tail fins of the period. Dodge called it Swept-Wing styling. Note jet-style tail lights and dual radio antennas.
73F : **Dodge** Sierra Series MD3-L Station Wagon, also available as Custom Sierra MD3-H. Six- and nine-passenger versions could be had, all with four doors and roll-down tailgate window.

74A Edsel Corsair

74D Ford Country Sedan

74E Ford Thunderbird

74B Ford Galaxie

74C Ford Fairlane 500

74A: **Edsel** 1959 range was revised and comprised three series: Corsair (4 models, four-door Hardtop shown), Ranger (4) and Villager Station Wagons (2). An OHV 223 CID 145-bhp six-cylinder engine was made available for Rangers and Villagers. Ford formed a new division, the Mercury-Edsel-Lincoln (M.E.L.) Division, but the 'E' was soon to be dropped: as a result of unexpectedly poor sales the Edsel line, after a final facelift for the 1960 model year, was discontinued in November 1959.

74B: **Ford** introduced new bodystyling and in addition to Custom 300, Fairlane and Fairlane 500 models there was a new top-line range named Galaxie. Compared here, the Galaxie Town Victoria, Model 75A, Fordor Hardtop in the foreground bore a strong resemblance to the contemporary Thunderbird, especially in the roof area.

74C: **Ford** Fairlane 500 Club Victoria, Model 63A, photographed at the Brussels World Fair with the 'Atomium' structure in the background. A four-door Hardtop, named Town Victoria was available also.

74D: **Ford** Country Sedans were available with six or nine seats (Models 71F and E resp.) and were among six models in the Station Wagon Series. Cargo space was 11 cubic feet greater than in 1958.

74E: **Ford** Thunderbird had revised radiator grille, and side ornaments ('bright metal spears on the side panel projectiles', Ford said). Hardtop version is shown here in front of the Place Belgique Reception Hall at the Brussels 'Expo' World Fair.

75A Imperial Crown

75B Lincoln

75C Mercury Monterey

75A: **Imperial** Crown MY1-M Southampton two-door Hardtop featured a stainless steel roof. In common with the DeLuxe MY1-L and LeBaron MY1-H it had 129-in wb and an improved 413 CID engine, developing 350 bhp at 4600 rpm. Auto.trans., PAB, PAS, reversing (back-up) lights, windscreen washers and dual exhausts were standard equipment. Air suspension (at rear) was optional.

75B: **Lincoln** offered Coupé, Landau (4-door Hardtop) and Sedan models in its regular (shown), Premiere and Continental lines. In addition there were Continental Convertible, Town Car and Limousine variants. All had 350-bhp 430 CID engine and 131-in wb. The Continental Mk IV Town Car and Limousine (with formal division) were ultra-luxurious motorcars, finished in 'Presidential Black'. Interiors featured subtle contrasts of grey broadcloth, black Scotch-grain leather and deep-piled carpeting. Standard equipment included air conditioning and other conveniences.

75C: **Mercury** celebrated its 20th anniversary and offered 15 new models in four series: Monterey, Montclair, Park Lane and Country Cruisers (station wagons). Shown: Monterey four-door Sedan, which, as standard, had a 312 CID 235-bhp power unit (280-bhp Marauder engine optional).

75D: **Mercury** Park Lane four-door Hardtop Cruiser. Note compound-curved windscreen and difference in roof styling with Monterey. Standard engine for Park Lanes was the 345-bhp Marauder V8. Wheelbase was 128 in (126 in for other series).

75E: **Meteor** was the Canadian-built Ford and came in a full range of body styles. Shown is the Rideau 500 four-door Sedan. Engine options: 145-bhp 223 CID Econ-O-Fuel Six or 225-bhp 332 CID or 303-bhp 361 CID Tempest V8s. Transmissions: 3-speed manual or 2-speed automatic Econ-O-Drive or dual-range Multi-Drive Merc-O-Matic, the latter for V8s only.

75F: **Monarch** Mark II was Ford of Canada's Mercury-based line and comprised 126-in wb Lucerne and Richelieu (shown) and 128-in wb Sceptre series, each with two- and four-door Cruiser Hardtop Sedans, as well as conventional sedans in the 126-in wb series. Engines: 280-bhp 383 CID V8 for Lucerne, 322-bhp 383 CID V8 for Richelieu, 345-bhp 430 CID V8 for Sceptre.

75D Mercury Park Lane

75E Meteor Rideau 500

75F Monarch Richelieu

76A: Metropolitan Convertible and Hardtop had several improvements, including outside trunk (boot) lid, side window vents, improved adjustable seats, larger tyres (5·20-13), etc. Austin of England, who made it for American Motors, called it the A50 Series IV and it was produced from 1959–61. From December 1956 until January 1959 and again during 1960–61 it was also marketed outside North America, as Austin Metropolitan 1500.

76B: Oldsmobile, like the other General Motors car-producing divisions, offered entirely new models with about 40 per cent more glass area and a new flat roof line for Holiday Sport Sedan four-door Hardtops. The latter body style was available in the 98 (shown), Super 88 and Dynamic 88 Series. Hydra-Matic was standard on the 98, optional on other Series. Air suspension was optional also.

76C: Oldsmobile Super 88 Holiday SceniCoupé was two-door hardtop coupé with extra large heat-resistant rear window which, like the Vista-Panoramic windscreen, contoured into the roofline. The 6·5-litre Rocket V8 developed 315 bhp.

76D: Oldsmobile Super 88 Fiesta Station Wagon had new roll-up rear window. As an optional extra, a power-operated rear window could be operated from both inside and outside.

76A Metropolitan

76C Oldsmobile Super 88

76B Oldsmobile Ninety-Eight

76D Oldsmobile Super 88

77A : **Plymouth** top-of-the-range car in 1959 was the Sport Fury, equipped with 260-bhp V8. Hardtop and Convertible (shown) models were available. Their front seats swivelled outward for ease of entry (optional on other Plymouths). A Golden Commando 361 CID engine with 10:1 CR and 305 bhp was optional. Series designations were MP1 for Sixes, MP2 for V8s.

77B : **Plymouth** Fury two-door Hardtop with Sport Deck and new outward-canted tail fins.

77C : **Plymouth** Fury four-door Hardtop Sedan. Also available as DeSoto Diplomat Custom and Dodge Kingsway Custom, but only for export.

77D : **Pontiac** Catalina Vista four-door Hardtop with Vista-Panoramic windscreen and large wrap-around rear window. Vista models were also available in the Bonneville and Star Chief Series. A wide range of V8 engine options was available.

77E : **Pontiac** six-cylinder models were produced by GM of Canada for domestic and export sales. Mechanically they had much in common with the Chevrolet, including the OHV Six engine (except for slightly larger bore) and optional Powerglide auto. trans. There were Strato Chief, Laurentian and Parisienne (two-door Hardtop shown) Series, all with 119-in wb.

77A Plymouth Sport Fury

77B Plymouth Fury

77C Plymouth Fury

77D Pontiac Catalina

77E Pontiac Parisienne (Canada)

1959

78A: **Rambler** American two-door Sedan continued virtually unchanged (see 1958) but Station Wagon variant, Model 5904, was new. It was available with either DeLuxe or Super trim and helped AMC to sell a record 368,464 cars during this year.

78B: **Rambler** Six Super Sedan, Model 5915-1, had 108-in wb and 127-bhp engine. Hardtops and Station Wagons were available also. All Ramblers, except the American, had four doors. Rebel models also had 108-in wb but 250 CID 215-bhp V8 engine.

78C: **Rambler** Ambassador Custom Country Club Hardtop, Model 5989-2, with 327 CID 270-bhp V8 and 117-in wb. The top-line

Ambassadors had a grille different in design from the 108-in wb Six and Rebel models.

78D: **Studebaker** completely revised their programme and concentrated on the new compact Lark ('striking a smart, sensible balance between the $\frac{5}{8}$ size European cars and the oversize US models') and the Silver Hawk (*q.v.*). In the Lark range there were two- and four-door Sedans, a two-door Hardtop and a Station Wagon. Shown is the Regal Hardtop. There was choice of engines : 90-bhp 169·6 CID L-head Six and 180- or 195-bhp 259·2 CID OHV V8. Wb of all Larks was 108·5 in, except Station Wagon, 113 in.

78A Rambler American

78C Rambler Ambassador

78B Rambler Six

78D Studebaker Lark

79A: **Studebaker** Silver Hawk had 120$\frac{1}{2}$-in wb and was offered with either flat-head Six or OHV V8. The supercharged engine was discontinued. This car measured 204 × 71$\frac{1}{4}$ × 56 in as against the Lark's 175 × 71$\frac{1}{2}$ × 57$\frac{1}{2}$ in.

79B: **Willys** introduced an additional model, aimed at fun-seeking Americans. Named Surrey it came complete with fringe on its canvas top and was gaily trimmed in a choice of colours: 'pink, green or blue candy stripes'. Basically it was a 4 × 2 Model DJ3A, fitted with chromium bumpers, wheel discs and other brightwork. It was similar to the Jeep Gala, a beach resort rental car, which was an export model.

79A Studebaker Silver Hawk

79B Willys Jeep

79C Chevrolet Corvair

The 'compacts' of the Big Three

In 1959 General Motors, Ford and Chrysler followed the lead of the 'independents' and introduced compact-sized cars, in addition to their large regular models. GM's entry was the revolutionary rear-engined Chevrolet Corvair, later the subject of Nader-inspired large-scale controversy in respect of safety. Chrysler's Plymouth dealers offered the sleek Valiant which, like Ford's Falcon, was of more conventional design.

79D Chrysler Plymouth Valiant

79E Ford Falcon

ABBREVIATIONS

AMA	Automobile Manufacturers Association, Inc.
AM, AMC	American Motors (Corporation)
auto.trans.	automatic transmission
bhp	brake horsepower*
carb.	carburettor
CID	cubic inch displacement (1 cu.in=16.39 cc)
CR	compression ratio
diff.	differential
Eight	eight-cylinder (engine)
F-head	inlet-over-exhaust-valve (engine)
GM	General Motors (Corporation)
hyd.	hydraulic
IFS	independent front suspension
in	inch (=2·54 cm)
L-head	side-valve (engine) (also known as flat-head)
OHV	overhead valves
PAB	power assisted brakes
PAS	power assisted steering
q.v.	quod vide (which see)
RHD	right-hand drive
rpm	revolutions per minute
SAE	Society of Automotive Engineers
Six	six-cylinder in line (engine)
V8	eight-cylinder in V-form (engine)
wb	wheelbase (distance between front and rear wheel centres)

*Until recently US manufacturers quoted gross bhp figures to SAE standards; these are used throughout this book and are higher than the actual output of the engines as installed in the vehicle.

SUMMARY OF MAJOR AMERICAN CAR MAKES, 1950-1959

AMERICAN MOTORS GROUP

Hudson	(1909–57)
Nash	(1917–57)
Rambler	(from 1956)

CHRYSLER GROUP

Chrysler	(from 1923)
Chrysler Imperial	(1926–54)
DeSoto	(1928–60)
Dodge	(from 1914)
Imperial	(from 1954)
Plymouth	(from 1928)

FORD GROUP

Edsel	(1957–59)
Ford	(from 1903)
Lincoln	(from 1920)
Mercury	(from 1938)
Meteor (Canada)	(from 1948)
Monarch (Canada)	(1946–61)

GENERAL MOTORS GROUP

Buick	(from 1903)
Cadillac	(from 1903)
Chevrolet	(from 1911)
Oldsmobile	(from 1896)
Pontiac	(from 1926)

OTHER MAKES

Checker	(from 1921)
Crosley	(1939–52)
Frazer	(1946–51)
Henry J	(1951–54)
Kaiser	(1946–55)*
Packard	(1899–1958)
Studebaker	(1902–66)**
Willys (-Overland)	(1908–63)

*later continued in Argentina
**horse-drawn vehicles from 1852

ACKNOWLEDGEMENTS

This book was compiled and written largely from historic source material in the library of the Olyslager Organisation. Additional photographs were kindly provided by American Motors, Chrysler, Ford and General Motors as well as several private collections, notably those of Jan Bakker and G. A. Ingram. Thanks are also extended to Gerard W. Hitman, David J. Voller and John M. Carpenter for valuable contributions and editorial comments.